Cenacle Sessions

A Modern Mystagogy

by
William R. Bruns

PAULIST PRESS
New York/Mahwah, N.J.

Cover art by Stella DeVenuta, O.S.F.

Library of Congress Cataloging-in-Publication Data

Bruns, William R., 1944-
  Cenacle sessions: a modern mystagogy/ William R. Bruns.
    p. cm.
  Includes bibliographical references.
  ISBN 0-8091-3249-4
    1. Initiation rites—Religious aspects—Catholic Church. 2. Catholic Church—Prayer-books and devotions—English. 3. Discipline of the secret. 4. Catholic Church Ordo initiationis Christianae adultorum. 5. Bible. N.T. John—Criticism, interpretation, etc.
BX2045.I55C46 1991
268'.434—dc20
                                                                    91-17142
                                                                    CIP

Published by Paulist Press
997 Macarthur Boulevard
Mahwah, New Jersey 07430

Printed and bound in the
United States of America

Contents

CONTENTS

8. Scripture Texts Used in the Sessions

To Alexa Suelzer, S.P., Ph.D.
Professor of Theology and Philosophy
Saint Mary-of-the-Woods College

Scholar, Master Teacher, and Friend

and to the Faculty and Administration
of Saint Mary-of-the-Woods College

whose steadfast belief in
Divine Providence
causes miracles to happen in our day

Preface

The title for this work has been carefully chosen to show the connection between our modern neophytes and the first disciples who (as traditional belief holds) continued to meet in the upper room—the cenacle—following the Good Friday-Easter Sunday experience.

It was in the cenacle that the disciples had celebrated the Lord's supper; it was in the cenacle that they first heard from the lips of Mary Magdalene: "I have seen the Lord!"; it was in the cenacle that they gathered to pray and to remember; it was in the cenacle that they experienced the presence of the risen Jesus; it was in the cenacle that they received power from on high; it was from the cenacle that they went forth on mission to evangelize and to minister.

Cenacle Sessions aims to provide a similar atmosphere and experience for today's new disciples.

The author of the fourth gospel, which is used exclusively in this mystagogy, set forth his purpose in these words:

> But these [signs of Jesus] are written that you may [come to] believe that Jesus is the messiah, the Son of God, and that through this belief you may have life in his name (Jn 20:31).

It is my hope that *Cenacle Sessions* will provide the vehicle through which John's purpose may be realized in our own day: that our neophytes may continue in their belief in Jesus as Christ and Lord and that they may be immersed in that source of life who is Jesus.

Praised be Jesus Christ!

William R. Bruns

1

1. Savoring the Mysteries

Mystagogy . . . is a time for deepening the Christian experience, for spiritual growth, and for entering more fully into the life and unity of the community.

(RCIA 7.4)

Mystagogy . . . is a time for the community and the neophytes together to grow in deepening their grasp of the paschal mystery and in making it part of their lives through meditation on the gospel, sharing in the eucharist, and doing works of charity. To strengthen the neophytes as they begin to walk in newness of life, the community of the faithful, their godparents, and their parish priests (pastors) should give them thoughtful and friendly help.

(RCIA 244)

The neophytes are, as the term "mystagogy" suggests, introduced into a fuller and more effective understanding of mysteries through the gospel message they have learned and above all through their experience of the sacraments they have received. For they have truly been renewed in mind, tasted more deeply the sweetness of God's word, received the fellowship of the Holy Spirit, and grown to know the goodness of the Lord. Out of this experience, which belongs to Christians and increases as it is lived, they derive a new perception of the faith, of the church, and of the world.

(RCIA 245)

Just as their new participation in the sacraments enlightens the neophytes' understanding of the scriptures, so too it increases their contact with the rest of the faithful and has an impact on the experience of the community. As a result, interaction between the neophytes and the faithful is made easier and more beneficial. The [mystagogia] is of great significance for both the neophytes and the rest of the faithful.

Through it the neophytes, with the help of their godparents, should experience a full and joyful welcome into the community and enter into closer ties with the other faithful. The faithful, in turn, should derive from it a renewal of inspiration and of outlook.

(RCIA 246)

After the immediate mystagogy . . . during the Easter season, the program for the neophytes should extend until the anniversary of Christian initiation, with at least monthly assemblies of the neophytes for their deeper Christian formation and incorporation into the full life of the Christian community.

(National [U.S.] Statutes for the Catechumenate, 24)

The call for the restoration of the ancient catechumenate was given to the church in 1962 in *Sacrosanctum Concilium* (*Constitution on the Sacred Liturgy*), the first document produced by the Second Vatican Council. Specific rites were not promulgated, however, until January 6, 1972, in the document *Ordo initiationis christianae adultorum* (*The Rite of Christian Initiation of Adults* [RCIA]). The full implementation of the process has been quite slow, especially in western, developed nations.

In the United States when the RCIA began to be used, it took the form—more often than not—of group instruction classes or "convert classes" to which public liturgical ceremonies were tacked on. For all the deficiencies in its implementation, however, the new approach was underway—not in the way the framers of the RCIA document had envisioned nor in a form recognizable to Cyril of Jerusalem, John Chrysostom, Ambrose, or Augustine. But at least attempts were being made to restore the catechumenate.

Thanks to the work of RCIA pioneers such as Christiane Brusselmans, James B. Dunning, James Lopresti, Ron Lewinski, Robert Duggan, Raymond B. Kemp, and a few others, the process of welcoming new Christians into the church began to take form in hundreds of parishes, where over the last decade it has been transformed into a reality much closer to the experience of the early church. These modern catechumenate "missionaries" insisted that the RCIA was a process and a sacramental rite, not merely an academic program, that it ultimately had more to do with conversion and formation than it did with intellectualization and information, and that it was a spiritual journey for both seekers and believers rather than a new way to approach adult education. Those involved in the direction of catechumenates listened, reacted, tried the "process approach," and usually became enthusiastic supporters.

However, nearly two decades have now passed since the promulgation of *Ordo initiationis christianae adultorum,* and there still remain gaps and weaknesses in the full implementation of the RCIA. All is not well with the RCIA process. This lassitude is perhaps most evident in the post-baptismal period—mystagogy—which just does not seem to be happening.

An Effort To Meet the Need

Cenacle Sessions: A Modern Mystagogy has been developed as an effort to answer the pastoral need for an effective mystagogy in today's church. Like the RCIA itself, *Cenacle Sessions* is designed to be flexible—adaptable—so that local communities can use it to match *their* pastoral situations.

History of the Mystagogy

Before discussing the details of *Cenacle Sessions,* it is necessary to come to some understanding of the role of mystagogy in the early church.

Developed in the early centuries of the present era, the mystagogy originally consisted of instructions to the newly baptized given daily during Easter week. At these gatherings, the neophytes heard homilies, usually delivered by the bishop, concerning the meaning of the sacramental actions in which they had participated at the Easter vigil.

The history of the development of mystagogy—like the history of the entire catechumenate—is sketchy. The process evolved in disparate geographical locations over long periods of time. What we do know of mystagogical catecheses is found in the texts of the homilies of the mystagogues themselves.

For instance, in A.D. 348 Cyril of Jerusalem delivered a series of mystagogic homilies (only five of which are still in existence) in a small chapel at the site of the Holy Sepulcher. Three of these instructions deal with baptism and chrismation (confirmation), one with eucharistic doctrine, and one with the eucharistic liturgy.

Often the mystagogical instructions also focused on the importance of sustaining the conversion experience. Some forty years after Cyril's mystagogy, in A.D. 389, John Chrysostom, recognizing that baptism and entrance into full communion with the church did not represent the end of the journey but only a milestone along the way, told the neophytes of the church of Constantinople:

> Imitate him [Christ] . . . I implore you, and you will be called *neophytes* not only for two, three, ten, or twenty days, but you will still merit this name after ten, twenty, or thirty years, and in fact for all of your lives (*Baptismal Catecheses*).

Challenges of Mystagogy Today

The modern church is having difficulties implementing an effective mystagogy. A natural lethargy seems to set in on clergy, catechumenate directors, catechists, parishioners, neophytes, and godparents following the rigorous and the oftentimes frenetic activities of Lent, Holy Week, and the Easter vigil. Everyone is tired (many would choose a stronger word here—perhaps *exhausted*).

The richness of the liturgical rites of the Easter vigil rightly communicates that this is the climax, the peak of the catechumenal journey; unfortunately, this high point is also often misunderstood as the destination and sole purpose of the journey. RCIA team members often reinforce this misperception by their actions or by their inaction, saying—intentionally or not—"You have arrived! It is over."

Often the very act of handing out typed schedules of the parish RCIA calendar—especially when the last item listed is the Easter vigil—sends a strong message to the neophytes that the celebration of the Easter sacraments is, in fact, their destination.

Pastoral staffs need to emphasize from the very first meeting that the journey of faith really is a journey and that there is no destination on this side of the grave. There may be rest stops, oases, and side trips, but only the Lord is the final destination. As Psalm 62 tells us: "In God alone there is rest for my soul." Augustine also pointed out in his *Confessions* that "our hearts are restless until they rest in you, Lord." Belonging to the church is a matter of always being restless, of always being on the move—on the move even *after* the Easter vigil.

Finally, one key element that gave rise to the need for a mystagogic period in the early church no longer exists. This key element was the *disciplina arcani,* the discipline of the secret.

The Discipline of the Secret

The term *mystagogy* was borrowed directly from the pagan mystery religions of the time and means literally a "leading through the mysteries." In the early days, the church observed the discipline of the secret, which required strict silence from believers concerning the rites and beliefs surrounding the initiation sacraments of baptism/chrismation and eucharist. The sacraments were called the mysteries then; they are referred to as *mysteries* in the Eastern Catholic and Orthodox churches to this day.

It was the discipline of the secret that barred outsiders from the assembly of the faithful and required catechumens and the elect to leave the worshiping assembly before the eucharist was celebrated. It was the discipline of the secret that gave that portion of the mass we now call the "liturgy of the word" its former name: "mass of the catechumens."

The discipline of the secret was probably enjoined on believers for two major reasons:

■ **Self-preservation:** Christianity was an illegal religion; its members were subject to persecution, including death. Therefore, extreme care was taken when admitting new members. Were they sincere believers or were they spies? If their conversions were sincere, would they be strong and deep, or would they apostatize at the first signs of persecution?

■ **Sound psychology and pedagogy:** Withholding certain pieces of information was intuitively recognized as good psychology and pedagogy. A fifth century bishop quotes Aristotle as saying, "Those undergoing initiation (in the mystery religions) are not expected to gain knowledge but an experience and a disposition."

It seems that the early bishops of the church, along with those involved in the pagan mystery cults, discovered the value of what we call today "experiential learning" techniques. The "awe-inspiring rites" (as Cyril of Jerusalem first referred to them) were to be experienced first, then reflected upon.

While some scholars suggest that the discipline of the secret was adopted directly from the pagan mystery cults and was the church's way of competing with them, this theory has been challenged regularly by other scholars. Whatever the actual genesis of the practice, the *disciplina arcani* created the need and constituted the very reason for the development and implementation of the mystagogy.

Contemporary liturgical theory is divided on the question of whether or not to prepare candidates for the initiation sacraments by explaining the rites, symbols, and liturgical actions in some detail prior to the ceremonies themselves. (One wonders whether our contemporary practice of catechizing children in preparation for their sacramental celebrations builds in a reflex that causes us to do the same thing with adults.)

At any rate, most parishes have already decided the question: the rites and meanings are explained—usually in some detail—beforehand. It is probably not reasonable to think that the majority of pastors, catechumenate directors, and catechists will "purify" their educational and liturgical theories by changing their method of sacramental catechesis. Additionally, it may not even be appropriate in today's church to adopt this practice just because it was done during the first six centuries of the church. The antiquity of a practice does not by any means make it automatically desirable today.

Purpose of the Modern Mystagogy

Regardless of which theories and practices eventually become normative in the church, we know two things for certain: the discipline of the secret no longer exists and catechesis on the mysteries prior to their celebration is commonplace today.

Both of these facts raise real questions concerning the appropriateness of mystagogy itself and the content of the mystagogic period:

- Is mystagogy still a relevant part of the initiation process?
- Has the church's contemporary experience of integrating newcomers rendered this ancient period of reflection obsolete?
- Are we expecting too much of modern-day neophytes?

Some parishes, tailoring the RCIA process to the nine or ten month school year, use the seven week Easter season to finish what properly ought to be have been the content of inquiry classes. (And this approach continues despite revised rites and mandated national statutes.) Others have used it as a time to evaluate the entire process—another signal to neophytes that "the journey is over." Others experience diminishing attendance during the Easter season as neophytes discover that the content of the sessions is without much substance. Still other parishes opt for only one or two gatherings during the Easter season, thus breaking the momentum and losing the regular contact that had been established during the catechumenate—and suffering a loss of participation.

As one who has worked with the RCIA process for a number of years, I believe that mystagogy is not only relevant but vital to the complete and effective initiation of new Christians. Our contemporary methods of implementing mystagogy (or, worse, our total disregard of this period of initiation) and the lack of substantial content for mystagogy have rendered this period ineffective and virtually useless.

It is pastorally important that mystagogy be implemented in effective ways because this period, as Robert Duggan has pointed out, is actually

> the gateway to the rest of life as a fully incorporated member of the church. If the RCIA is to be an instrument of substantial, lasting reform and renewal of parish life, then the mystagogy will have to play a crucial role in establishing the pattern according to which conversion will be lived over and over by each and every member of the community. ("Mystagogy and Continual Conversion: RCIA Success Stories," *Christian Initiation Resources Reader.* Vol. IV: *Mystagogia and Ministries,* 1984, p. 30.)

During the inquiry and catechumenal periods, RCIA teams are very careful to see that community is built, fellowship is extended, and tender, loving care is given. These aspects of the process are universally recognized as vital and important. How is it then that we abandon the neophytes at our baptismal fonts and immersion pools?

Need for a Modern Mystagogy

Here lies the source of *Cenacle Sessions.* Here lies the impetus to develop an effective mystagogy for our time. An effective mystagogy is called for because our new sisters and brothers, still wet with the life-giving baptismal waters and still enveloped with the sweet fragrance of the holy chrism, are often left alone, each to find his or her own way into the fabric of the life of our parishes. And many are not able to find that way by themselves.

If mystagogy serves no other purpose than that of softening for the neophytes the psychological shock of being forced out of the catechu-

menal nest and of integrating them easily into the community, then
such a process not only is a "nice" way to bridge this transitional
period but is a necessity demanded by Christian love and concern.

Defining a Modern Mystagogy

Today, in the absence of the discipline of the secret and with the
practice of catechizing the elect about the "mysteries" before they
experience the sacraments, we seem to have no real reason for "leading
our neophytes through the mysteries" after Easter. Still, we recognize
that there is a definite need for a reflective, transitional, integrative
process to help neophytes adjust to their new identities. How, then, are
we to define a modern mystagogy?

I propose that a twentieth century American mystagogy should be
defined and understood as simply this:

a savoring time.

A modern mystagogy should be a time used not so much for
explication as for meditation, not so much for tying up loose ends as
for tying bonds of love to the neophytes, and not so much a time of
signing up neophytes for this or that ministry as for exploring with
them the life of service into which they have so recently been born.

A modern mystagogy is a time to savor the marvelous things the
Lord has accomplished in the individual lives of the neophytes and in
the corporate life of the faith community.

A modern mystagogy is a time to savor the gifts of the new
members and to help them find their individual places—places to
which the Lord is beckoning them and in which they are being asked to
exercise their gifts.

A modern mystagogy is a time to savor the neophytes' experiences of the initiation mysteries, which the western church calls
sacraments.

A modern mystagogy is a time to savor the mystery that the neophytes are becoming, the mystery that is church.

The Process in General

We need to let everyone involved in the RCIA—from catechists
to pastors—know that it's natural to be tired on Easter Monday and

that it really is okay to take time to rest. After all, we have just spent the last forty days in intense labor, bringing forth this new life: we have all given birth to new Christians.

In addition, if we really come to understand mystagogy as a savoring time, we also need to complete that image by realizing that intelligent diners do not arise quickly from the table after a fine meal and return to work or to business as usual—diners take the time to savor their meal. We, too, need to take time to savor our experiences. Savoring time is an essential part of any meal; it should be an essential part of life.

For this reason, *Cenacle Sessions* begins by savoring the Easter season principally through quiet reflection—both private and public —on the gospels and by participation in the community's eucharist on the Lord's day. A neophyte's journal, *Easter Bread,* developed as a part of *Cenacle Sessions,* provides the new Christians with a structured method of reflecting on the Sunday gospels of Easter.

Suggestions are given in this mystagogue's guide for the very visible involvement of the neophytes in the Lord's day eucharists of Eastertide. The neophytes themselves are, after all, important "sacraments" for the church during this season.

In the summer months following Pentecost, the pastor, mystagogue, or catechumenate director should convene the neophytes for informal social gatherings: a picnic, a day-long outing to a local monastery or convent, a midsummer's eve cookout, an outdoor concert, a July 4 fireworks display, a parish softball game.

In August the neophytes should begin meeting with the mystagogue to savor what they experienced during the previous Lent and at the Easter vigil. One of the seven *Cenacle Sessions* is meant to be held about once a month during the remainder of the neophytes' first year as fully initiated Christians. Each session is structured to include a period of prayer, a time of remembering the ritual experiences of the RCIA, input from the mystagogue, and a discussion or group process activity.

The heart of these sessions consists of calling upon each person's power of memory and linking those memories to the RCIA Lenten rites and to selections from the gospel of John, a gospel that many scholars believe was written—at least in part—for the newly baptized of the late first century.

Many scholars believe that the author of the fourth gospel put his experiences of Jesus into writing because of his concern that the deeper message and cosmic meaning of Jesus as word, Lord, and source of

Life were being lost to neophytes and to their communities with the passage of time and with the dying of the last of the witnesses who had known Jesus in the flesh and as risen Lord prior to his return to the Father.

Setting, Environment

Ideally, the group (or groups) of neophytes should be convened in a home (or at least in a non-classroom, non-institutional setting), and not more than two-thirds of the group should consist of neophytes. The balance of the group should comprise members of the neophytes' new faith community. The hope here is that these sessions will help introduce the neophytes to more members of the local faith community, thus establishing relationships that will alleviate the abandoned-at-the-font syndrome. The mixed membership will also help the group serve as a "training ground" for members of the community who might be interested in serving as mystagogues or as members of the RCIA team in future years.

The cenacle has come to be understood as the upper room of the last supper and of the descent of the Holy Spirit. The simple meaning of the word *cenacle,* however, is "a small dining room usually on an upper floor of a house." It seems appropriate, then, that we call this particular modern mystagogical savoring process *Cenacle Sessions.*

2. A Mystagogic Calendar

The flexibility and adaptability found in the RCIA are built into the design of *Cenacle Sessions.* I have tried not to create another "program." Rather, I hope that *Cenacle Sessions* presents a way of looking at, an approach to, mystagogy—with a few specific ideas presented as a means of grasping the bigger picture.

How *Cenacle Sessions* is best implemented is left to the pastoral wisdom of the ministers of each community. Individual needs and concerns unique to each community will (and should) dictate the detailed implementation of that community's mystagogy.

The calendar suggested here presents one approach that meets the U.S. bishops' wishes that the post-baptismal period last for one year. Each community should consider this calendar merely as a starting point for designing a mystagogy that fits its individual needs and the needs of the larger church.

During Eastertide

Relaxation, reflection, and the joy of awesome wonder in new life should mark this period. Neophytes and their companions on the journey should spend time reflecting on the Lord's day gospels of this season. Ideally this should be done during the week prior to each Sunday's liturgical celebration.

Some neophytes may wish to continue meeting each week to break open and share the word. This approach is optional; it should not be expected. Do not minimize the need for everyone to rest and for everyone to have unscheduled time during this season.

Some neophytes may wish to meet with their godparents or with some other significant journeyer. Other neophytes may want to further integrate the word into their prayer lives through private meditation and reflection. The RCIA director, a competent catechist, or the mystagogue should provide the necessary instruction on how to accomplish this if such has not been dealt with during the catechumenate or enlightenment periods.

A neophyte journal, *Easter Bread,* has been designed as a companion publication that will facilitate either group or private reflection on the gospels of the Easter season.

Lord's Day Masses of the Easter Season

As called for in the RCIA and in the catechumenal statutes for the United States, the neophytes, their godparents, and those who have journeyed with them should continue to be present as a group at the community's principal eucharistic liturgy each Sunday during the Easter season. Suggestions regarding their involvement appropriate to the Sunday are given in the next chapter, "Lord's Day Eucharists During Eastertide."

Mystagogy Following the Easter Season

The balance of the year (from the Monday after Pentecost until the following Easter vigil or celebration of the first anniversary of the neophytes' baptisms) is devoted to monthly gatherings with a mystagogue. These gatherings are designed to:

■ further deepen the neophytes' understanding of the paschal mystery;
■ clarify their relationship to, and their lives within, the church community;
■ recall for them their sacramental experiences during the preceding Lent and triduum.

The Mystagogic Year

Because the date for the celebration of Easter varies from year to year, it will be necessary to adjust this calendar, which has been constructed under the assumption that Easter will fall in early April.

APRIL

Easter Vigil
    Celebration of the initiation sacraments

APRIL/MAY

Seven Weeks of Eastertide
    Private or group reflection on the Sunday gospels using *Easter Bread*

Seven Sundays of Easter
    Participation in the community's principal eucharistic liturgy

JUNE
(Begin monthly meetings)

Picnic, parish picnic, RCIA cookout, outdoor mass

JULY

Independence Day celebration, visit to an amusement park, ice cream social, parish softball game, social with new inquirers

AUGUST

Cenacle Session I: Called and Chosen

SEPTEMBER

Cenacle Session II: Sight and Insight

OCTOBER

Cenacle Session III: Light and Life

NOVEMBER

Cenacle Session IV: Water and Spirit

DECEMBER

Advent Prayer Service for Neophytes, "Gaudeamus" (Advent Party)

JANUARY

Cenacle Session V: Bread and Life

FEBRUARY

Cenacle Session VI: Love and Commitment

MARCH

Cenacle Session VII: Power and Peace

APRIL

Celebration of the Easter sacraments with the community and the new neophytes, anniversary celebration with the newly baptized (or separately)

3. Lord's Day Eucharists During Eastertide

During the period immediately after baptism, the faithful should take part in the masses for neophytes, that is, the Sunday masses of the Easter season . . . welcome the neophytes with open arms in charity, and help them to feel more at home in the community of the baptized.

(RCIA 9.5)

On all the Sundays of the Easter season after Easter Sunday, the so-called masses for the neophytes are to be scheduled. The entire community and the newly baptized with their godparents should be encouraged to participate. . . .

(RCIA 25)

Since the distinctive spirit and power of the period of post-baptismal catechesis or mystagogy derive from the new, personal experience of the sacraments and of the community, its main setting is the so-called masses for neophytes, that is, the Sunday masses of the Easter season. Besides being occasions for the newly baptized to gather with the community and share in the mysteries, these celebrations include particularly suitable readings from the lectionary, especially the readings for Year A. Even when Christian initiation has been celebrated outside the usual times, the texts for these Sunday masses of the Easter season may be used.

(RCIA 247)

All the neophytes and their godparents should make an effort to take part in the masses for the neophytes and the entire local community should be invited to participate with them. Special places in the congregation are to be reserved for the neophytes and their godparents. The homily and, as circum-

stances suggest, the general intercessions should take into
account the presence and needs of the neophytes.

(RCIA 248)

To close the period of post-baptismal catechesis, some sort of
celebration should be held at the end of the Easter season
near Pentecost Sunday; festivities in keeping with local custom may accompany the occasion.

(RCIA 249)

Here are some suggestions for involving the neophytes in visible,
meaningful ways in the Lord's day eucharists of the Easter season. The
rite itself suggests the use of the Cycle A readings for those masses at
which the neophytes are present. However, an examination of the
gospels indicates that common messages are proclaimed on these Easter Sundays regardless of the lectionary cycle. For example, the gospels
for the Third Sunday of Easter deal with table companionship in all
three cycles, and the gospels for the Fourth Sunday of Easter all focus
on the good shepherd motif.

While the readings from the Acts of the Apostles during the Easter
season present a dramatic vision of mission, and while it is extremely
tempting to treat each of the readings of Eastertide as a potential meditation for the neophytes and their companions, the approach of *Cenacle Sessions* deliberately concentrates on the gospels because they
seem to be the most realistic focal point for the post-baptismal savoring time. For this reason, too, *Easter Bread,* the companion volume to
Cenacle Sessions, concentrates exclusively on the Easter gospel selections as food for thought for the neophytes. The following are some
practical suggestions for each Sunday of the Easter season.

The Second Sunday of Easter:
Believing In Order To See

The gospel is John 20:19–31: Thomas the doubter. Both old and
new Christians should be strengthened with the words of Jesus in this
passage: "Have you come to believe because you have seen me?
Blessed are those who have not seen and have believed."

Ask one or two volunteers from among the neophytes to address
the assembly on Sunday and briefly tell the congregation how they

came to believe without seeing Jesus (or did they, in fact, see Jesus in members of the church and of the parish?). How do they feel about being new members of the church and the parish?

The Third Sunday of Easter:
Bread and Fish—Table Companionship

The gospel for all three cycles deals with Jesus being recognized at table—Emmaus (A), a fish supper in the cenacle (B), a breakfast of bread and fish on the shore of the Sea of Tiberias (C).

Ask the neophytes to take up a second collection for the homeless and the hungry or ask them to help organize the collection of canned goods at all the masses. Have them present the gifts, including the money or canned goods, at the preparation of the gifts.

Or ask one or two neophytes to address the assembly and tell the people of their feelings about and appreciation of the mass and their feelings about finally being able to share in the table of the eucharist.

The Fourth Sunday of Easter:
Good Shepherd Sunday

Prior to this "Good Shepherd Sunday," the mystagogue might ask members of the group to identify a church organization or group that they believe is "feeding the lambs and tending the sheep."

Depending on what type of group is identified, agree to take some appropriate action to help, support, or recognize the group for its work.

An example: The neophytes decide that the parish's educational ministers (board of education members, administrators, teachers, catechists) do a fine job of feeding and tending. They agree to write them a letter of appreciation to be read (with the presider's permission) at the announcement time at the liturgy.

Another example: If the group collected money or food on the Third Sunday of Easter, ask one of the neophytes to render a report to the assembly prior to the beginning of the liturgy or at the announcement time regarding the disposition of the food or money.

The Fifth Sunday of Easter:
Ministries in the Community

Ask one of the neophytes to tell the congregation how one or more of the community's ministers/ministries touched him or her and helped influence the neophyte's decision to join the church and this particular community.

After mass the neophytes might wish to join parish leaders in staffing tables in the parish hall for a Ministry Fair, where they would help the leaders answer questions from parishioners about the various parish organizations and activities and encourage the involvement of all parishioners in some aspect of the community's life and mission.

The Sixth Sunday of Easter:
A Community of Love

The gospel selections in all cycles are taken from the prayer of Jesus at the last supper; they deal with the fact that the community of Jesus Christ is to be a community of love. It is the love of the sisters and the brothers that is a reflection of the inner life of the Holy Trinity: perfect love, perfect unity among Father, Son, and Spirit.

Here are several options for the involvement of the neophytes in this liturgy:

■ Following the penitential rite, ask the presider to introduce the idea that today's gospel shows Jesus praying and speaking about the love and friendship that should exist among his followers. In large parishes it is often difficult to know each other's names, much less to consider each other as friends. Point out that your community's newest members are present and ask members of the assembly to introduce themselves to a neophyte they haven't had a chance to meet, or to someone else they do not know.

■ Ask one or more of the neophytes to address the assembly following the homily (and as a sort of postscript to it) and tell them how love and friendship influenced them to join this particular community.

■ If your parish is not too large: after an appropriate homily, call the neophytes forth, ask them to kneel in the front of the church building, and then invite members of the assembly (or parish council officers, and/or leaders of parish organizations, renewal groups, prayer groups, etc.) to come forth and lay hands on them as a symbol of friendship, welcome, unity, and incorporation.

■ At the sign of peace, ask the presider to call the neophytes forth and extend to each of them a very special and individual sign of peace. Then have the neophytes "pass the peace" to members of the assembly.

The Seventh Sunday of Easter:
The Priestly Prayer of Jesus

Again, in all three cycles, the gospel selections for this Sunday concentrate on the prayer of Jesus at the last Supper: "Father, give glory to your Son" (A); "Consecrate my followers in the truth" (B); "May all be one in us" (C).

Since it is through baptism and confirmation that we become priests of the new covenant, work with the parish liturgy commission and the pastor to have the neophytes assist the presider in a *Vidi Aquam* (sprinkling) rite at mass.

Point out to the congregation that the neophytes, as those in the community who most recently have been touched by the life-giving waters of baptism and have been anointed with the holy chrism, are the parish's newest "priests" and, therefore, are very appropriate individuals to assist the community's ordained priest in this rite.

Pentecost: The Descent of the Holy Spirit

Because this Sunday closes the Easter season, this will be the last opportunity for the neophytes to assemble and worship as a group within the community. Now they are to be "sent forth" into the faith community and beyond—sent forth to serve.

Ask the parish hosts/greeters/ushers to hand out small wax tapers to all those who enter the church for Sunday eucharist.

As the musicians play a gathering song, have the neophytes, holding lighted candles, enter from the rear of the church and proceed toward the sanctuary by the side aisles (so as to "encircle" the assembly). When they are in place, have them turn toward the center aisle. The musicians begin the opening song and the assembly stands. At this point, the presider and liturgical ministers may process down the middle aisle.

After the greeting, the presider explains in a few words the significance of the candle-bearing neophytes. The presider might wish to mention that John Chrysostom (fourth century) referred to the newly baptized as new lights. This was, in Greek, a play on the word *neophytos* (neophytes), which means new plants or seedlings. Chrysostom changed the second half of the compound word from *-phytos* (plants) to *-phos* (light). The presider should then invite the neophytes to extinguish their candles and take their seats.

During the homily, the preacher might render an account of the community's Ministry Fair that was held on the Fifth Sunday of Easter: how many people attended, how many new "ministers" stepped forth to assume various tasks in the community, etc.

After the homily the neophytes are called forth by name and approach the altar where they sign a promise to be involved in the community in a specified way. (Each neophyte has prayed about and discerned his or her involvement with a companion prior to this time.)

At the dismissal the neophytes are again called forth from the assembly. They approach the lighted Easter candle, light their tapers, and stand before the alter facing the presider.

When all are assembled, the presider gives the neophytes a solemn blessing, "missioning" or "sending forth." After receiving the blessing, the neophytes go into the assembly and light the small tapers of all the members of the congregation as they may have done at the Easter vigil.

When all candles are lit, the presider exhorts the congregation to allow the Holy Spirit to fill them with its presence and to let the light of the Spirit shine forth in service. The presider then blesses the assembly and dismisses everyone.

The closing hymn of the mass is sung. At its conclusion, the presider and ministers process out, extinguishing their candles only upon leaving the church.

Plan a special celebration—coffee and rolls following this mass, a picnic, a reception after an anticipated mass or at the last mass of Sunday—to bring the Easter season to a festive close.

4. The Monthly Sessions in General

Suggestions for the Mystagogue

Cenacle Sessions assumes:

■ that the catechumenate director and members of the RCIA team have worked diligently at all stages of the rite to build community among all persons involved in the RCIA.

■ that an understanding exists among all members of the RCIA team that becoming a Catholic Christian is an ongoing process, a rite, a sacrament; it is *not* a *program.* A program has an end. The RCIA has no end. And it certainly doesn't end at the Easter vigil.

■ that from the very beginning, schedules distributed to neophytes and others list the mystagogy as an integral part of the RCIA.

■ that faith-sharing and personal storytelling have been experienced by the neophytes and members of the team before they arrive at mystagogy. Those communities that dismiss their elect after the liturgy of the word and reconvene them in a separate place to "break open the word" will be well on their way to a fruitful mystagogy.

Not Scripture Study

Cenacle Sessions is not meant to be a Bible study. It is designed to give neophytes the time and opportunity to reflect upon what has happened to them during their journey toward membership in the Catholic Church. The scripture selections from the gospel of John are used as vehicles to facilitate that reflection process. Coming to know and understand the details of John's gospel are not the goals of *Cenacle Sessions;* the use of the Johannine gospel is but the means to the larger goal: savoring the moments of the journey.

Dealing with Miscellaneous Questions

It is important to take time in each session to deal with the "miscellaneous questions" that will be cropping up among the neophytes.

If these questions are ignored, the neophytes' minds will be focused on the questions instead of on the topic at hand.

A reasonable amount of time spent on questions such as "Why do Catholics have religious medals blessed?" or "Why do Catholics pray with their eyes open?" or other such questions that for one reason or another were never asked or answered during the inquiry period is not "wasted time." It clears the minds of the neophytes, it aids the ongoing insertion of the neophytes into the community (sharing group knowledge), and it can serve as social "small talk" that can lighten the heavier discussion of the evening.

Discussion Starters

The suggested questions listed for each session are meant to be discussion starters. Your group may use all of them; it may use only one of them; it may use none of them. The task is not to "answer the questions." The task at hand is to discuss "The Remembering" aided by the scripture selection for each session.

If the dialogue is going well and someone in the group suggests, "Let's go on to the next question or we'll never get finished," please assure the participants that there is no reason to hurry: "Let's just relax and see where our discussion takes us."

You may wish to avoid distributing a list of the questions to participants. Experience has shown that this tends to inhibit dialogue and to raise the stress levels of the neophytes who want to be certain to give the "right answers."

One mystagogue has found it effective to send one or more of the questions to various participants about one week before the group is scheduled to meet. You may wish to enclose a note:

> Dear John:
>
> As I was preparing our next *Cenacle Sessions* meeting, I thought of this question and how it relates to your experience: _____ Would you be good enough to give it some thought and be ready to talk about it next Wednesday evening when the group meets? Thanks a lot.
>
> Mary

The Role of Memory

The ability to remember is one of the truly magnificent powers that human beings possess. Through memory we can actually make present persons and events that exist only in the past. Through memory, people and places that we have once known can become present for us even though we might be separated from them by several thousand miles. "Memory," as musician-composer-poet Carey Landry has said, "is the sacrament of presence."

Memory is a hierophany, a door to the sacred. It has the ability to transport us into a sacred space that is different from the space we ordinarily occupy, into a sacred time that is different from ordinary time, into a world of sacred meaning through which the ordinary becomes profoundly enwrapped within the extraordinary.

Memory, because of its sacramentality, serves a valid and vital function in religion. Christianity, for example, employs the power of memory in a special way in its central sacrament, the eucharist. "Do this in memory of me," Jesus told his disciples. Through this anamnesis—this sacred memorial remembering—those actions that Jesus performed at the last supper are made present to us. We not only remember them, but we remember them in such a way that they become really present to us. Ordinary time becomes sacred time; ordinary space becomes sacred space; ordinary meaning becomes sacred meaning. Such is the power of memory.

In *Cenacle Sessions,* the use of memory is central to the mystagogic process. In each session there is a time called "The Remembering." Since we have defined mystagogy as a savoring time, we call upon our power of memory to recall, to recollect, to recapture, to enable us to relive those important sacramental moments of initiation—moments that we wish to bring out of storage in the past, as it were, and reexperience. We do this so that those moments may, in fact, be savored and so that their deeper meanings may become apparent to neophytes and companions alike.

For this reason, it is imperative that the mystagogue has witnessed the sacramental moments that she or he will call forth during "The Remembering" at each session. If the mystagogue has not been present, "The Remembering" should be facilitated by one who was there, an eyewitness.

The actual facilitation of "The Remembering" will, of course, reflect the personality and approach of each mystagogue. The following suggestions are offered, however, as an aid to that facilitation:

■ Make every attempt to see that the participants are interiorly quiet before beginning "The Remembering." The use of music greatly aids this phase. Do not rush the music. Spending five or even ten minutes with the music is recommended.

■ Speak in a quiet and unhurried manner. Do not disrupt the quiet centeredness achieved by the group.

■ Employ detailed and descriptive language. The more accurately you can portray the event, the more vivid will be the memories. You are painting a picture here. Paint with the colors, sights, sounds, smells, mood, and tone of the event.

■ Try to walk through the event orally in an orderly and chronological manner. If you remember the event in a similar sequence as the participants do, it will aid their remembering of it.

"The Remembering" calls upon all your gifts as storyteller, poet, and guide. Use those gifts freely.

Suggestions for Music

If possible, the mystagogue should work with an accomplished liturgical musician to choose and lead the music during *Cenacle Sessions.* Generally speaking, it is always preferable to sing the music rather than to listen to recorded music. However, if the music that is appropriate for the occasion calls for gifts beyond those possessed by you or by others involved, then by all means use recorded music.

Music is vital to this process. Do not dispense with the use of music just because you yourself do not have musical abilities, because a pastoral musician is not available, or because arranging for music seems to be too much trouble. In general, music is important because it sets the tone and establishes a prayerful atmosphere. Music is an irreplaceable element of *Cenacle Sessions* because, like our sense of smell, it is one of our most powerful memory triggers. It will greatly facilitate the effectiveness of "The Remembering."

The music suggested here is anything but exhaustive; it has been chosen because it is familiar to American Catholics and should be easily accessible to most parishes. Most of the selections can also be rendered simply, generally with guitar accompaniment. You are encouraged, however, to make the music your own.

Selections for General Use

Abba! Father!	Landry (NALR)
Amazing Grace	Traditional
Are Not Our Hearts	Landry (NALR)

Come, Holy Ghost	Traditional
Companions on the Journey	Landry (NALR)
Dwelling Place	Foley (NALR)
Father, We Adore You	Coelho (Maranatha Evangelical Assoc.)
For You Are My God	Foley (NALR)
Gather Us In	Haugen (GIA Publishing, Inc.)
Hallelujah, Our God Reigns	Garratt (Scripture in Songs Recordings Ltd)
Let Us Sing	Holtz (The Word of God)
Our God Reigns	Smith (Leonard E. Smith, Jr.)
Peace Is Flowing Like a River	Traditional
Sing a New Song	Schutte (NALR)
Sing to the Mountains	Dufford (NALR)
This Day God Gives Me	Traditional
We Remember	Haugen (GIA)
We've Been to the Mountain	McAllister (World Library)

Session I: Called and Chosen

Anthem	Conry (NALR)
By Name I Have Called You	Landry (NALR)
We Are the Branches	Miffleton (World Library)
We Walk by Faith	Haugen (GIA)

Session II: Sight and Insight

Amazing Grace	Traditional
Lay Your Hands	Landry (NALR)
Pardon Your People	Landry (NALR)
Veni, Sancte Spiritus	Berthier (Taizé)

Session III: Light and Life

Christ Our Light	(from the Easter Vigil)
Let There Be Light!	Traditional (Italian Hymn) also known as Come, Our Almighty King
Let Us Walk in the Light	Haugen (GIA)
The Lord Is My Light	Haas (GIA)

Session IV: Water and Spirit

Born Again	Fortunate (J. S. Paluch Company, Inc.)
Come to the Water	Foley (NALR)
The Lights of the City	Traditional (arrangmt. Guttfreund)
There Is One Lord	Taizé
You Have Been Baptized	Landry (NALR)

Session V: Bread and Life

Give Thanks and Remember	Miffleton (World Library)
I Am the Bread of Life	Toolan (GIA)
In Memory of Jesus	Landry (NALR)
Look Beyond	Ducote (Damean Music)
One Bread, One Body	Foley (NALR)
We Remember	Haugen (GIA)

Session VI: Love and Commitment

Anthem	Conry (NALR)
Be Not Afraid	Dufford (NALR)
City of God	Schutte (NALR)
Do You Really Love Me?	Landry (NALR)
Here I Am, Lord	Schutte (NALR)
Make Us True Servants	Traditional (Paluch)

Session VII: Power and Peace

City of God	Schutte (NALR)
Come, Holy Ghost	Traditional
Let There Be Light!	Traditional (Italian Hymn) also known as Come, Our Almighty King
Make Us True Servants	Traditional (Paluch)
The Spirit Is A-Movin'	Landry (NALR)
Veni, Sancte Spiritus	Berthier (Taizé)

5. Individual Sessions

SESSION I:
CALLED AND CHOSEN

SUGGESTED USE OF TIME

7:30   Introductions
7:45   Introduction of the Mystagogy
8:15   Prayer
8:30   Refreshments
8:45   Dialogue
9:25   Closing Prayer
9:30   Dismissal

Environment:

You may wish to consider having vining plants, such as philoden-drons, arranged as a centerpiece in the meeting room. Additionally, you may wish to have on hand some newly rooted individual vines that participants could take home with them to plant and watch grow.

INTRODUCTIONS (15 minutes)

Introduce yourself if everyone does not clearly know you. Ask all the participants to introduce themselves and suggest that each person identify himself or herself as a new member of the church, a sponsor, a parish member, etc.

INTRODUCTION OF THE MYSTAGOGY (30 minutes)

Introduce the concept of *Cenacle Sessions* (see Chapter 1). Em-phasize that these sessions are *not* a scripture study, but that the use of the scriptures continues to be the best way of deepening our faith commitment and of strengthening our relationships with the Lord and with one another.

Explain to participants the general outline of the sessions:
- Prayer
- The Remembering (see Chapter 4)
- Scripture
- Dialogue
- Simple refreshments, socializing

PRAYER (15 minutes)

Note: It is assumed that the mystagogue is the prayer leader. While this is not absolutely necessary, it would probably be wise for the first few sessions to set the tone and pace and to guide participants in "The Remembering."

Opening Song:

See "Suggestions for Music" in Chapter 4.

Opening Prayer:

Spontaneous by mystagogue (always *prepared* spontaneity, of course).

The Remembering:

Recall for the participants the *Rite of Sending for Election/Recognition* as it was celebrated in your parish as well as the Rite of Election/Call to Continuing Conversion as it was celebrated with your bishop in the cathedral church (or as a deanery or vicariate if that is your custom) this past Lent. Elements you may wish to bring to mind:

Rite of Sending for Election/Recognition
- Being called by name from out of the assembly
- The response of the catechumens, godparents, candidates, sponsors
- Signing of the Book of the Elect by the catechumens
- Music that has come to be special to the neophytes—perhaps a recurring hymn used throughout Lent or the catechumenate or a spe-

cial piece used at this particular rite (you may wish to use this as the music at the beginning of the prayer time)

- The reaction of the congregation.

Rite of Election/Call to Continuing Conversion
- Being present for the first time in the cathedral church or in an assembly with the bishop presiding
- Hearing your name announced
- Being welcomed and accepted by the bishop and the larger church

Ask participants to try to bring to mind their feelings at that rite: anxiety, eagerness, joy, fear, happiness, tearfulness, being deeply touched, etc.

Allow silent time or time with music playing.

Scripture Reading:

John 15:1–17

Prayers of Petition or Thanksgiving:

Voice one or two prayers yourself; then invite spontaneous prayers from the participants.

Closing Song:

See suggestions in Chapter 4.

REFRESHMENTS (15 minutes)

DIALOGUE (40 minutes)

Here are possible discussion starter questions. Your group may use all of them; you may use one of them; you may use none of them. The task is not to answer the questions. The task at hand is to discuss "The Remembering" and the scripture.

1. What was your predominant feeling during "The Remembering"?
2. What symbolic action from the Rite of Election/Call to Continuing Conversion spoke most powerfully to you? Why?
3. What did it mean to you to move from the status of catechumen to that of elect? (If some members of the group had already been baptized: What did it mean to you to be publicly recognized by the church and exhorted to live in deeper conformity to the life of Christ?)
4. How did you feel about that designation: *elect?*
5. In the scripture reading, Jesus describes himself as the vine and his followers as the branches. What do you think he was trying to tell us in that metaphor?
6. Jesus told his followers that they didn't choose him, but that he chose them. Do you feel chosen by the Lord?
7. Who chooses whom?
8. Are there people who never get chosen by Jesus?
9. In the scripture reading, Jesus told his followers that he would call them *friends.* Is that a word you would use to describe your relationship with Jesus? Why? If not, what word would best describe your relationship with him?
10. What does it really mean in the church "to love one another"? What do you think is *really* required of us on a day-to-day practical level?
11. Do you believe that we are required to lay down our lives for each other? What does that mean?

CLOSING PRAYER (5 minutes)

You may wish to close with a spontaneous prayer, to adopt a common prayer to recite, or to sing a song together at the end of each session. If you have vines for participants, you may wish to give the vines to them at this time.

DISMISSAL

SESSION II:
SIGHT AND INSIGHT

SUGGESTED USE OF TIME

7:30   Prayer
8:15   Refreshments
8:30   Dialogue
9:25   Closing Prayer
9:30   Dismissal

Environment:

Use an attractive urn, decanter, or cruet of olive oil as a central symbol for this session. Also have on hand a small bowl into which you can pour the oil during the prayer and from which you will anoint the participants.

PRAYER (45 minutes)

Opening Song:

See suggestions in Chapter 4.

Opening Prayer:

Spontaneous by the mystagogue.

The Remembering:

Recall for participants one or more of the scrutinies (celebrated with the catechumens) or the penitential rite (celebrated with candidates for reception) during Lent. If, during the catechumenate period, your parish celebrated the presentation of the creed or the anointing of the catechumens with the oil of catechumens, you may wish to recall those events. Particular elements you may wish to bring to mind:

Scrutinies/Penitential Rite
- Kneeling (bowing) during the prayers of exorcism
- The exorcism prayers themselves
- The laying on of hands
- Special music

Presentation of the Creed (Elect):
- The receiving of the creed
- The giving back (reciting, handing back a scroll, etc.) of the creed
- Special music

Celebrating the Sacrament of Reconciliation for the First Time (Candidates)
- Confessing sins to the priest—face to face or anonymously
- The experience of forgiveness
- Special music

Anointing with the Oil of Catechumens (Catechumens)
- The feel of the oil on your skin
- The prayers of the presider
- Special music

Ask the participants to try to bring to mind their feelings at these rites: fear, relief, joy, acceptance, forgiving, being forgiven, healing . . .

Scripture Reading:

John 9:1–41

Anointing:

Background music is suggested during the following anointing ceremony. "Veni, Sancte Spiritus" (Taizé) is especially appropriate and works well.

Mystagogue:

Slowly pour some of the oil into the bowl. Then, extending one or both hands over the oil say the following or similar prayer:

God, my Lord Almighty, the Father of our Lord and Savior Jesus Christ, stretch out your hand upon the fruit of the olive with which you anointed the priests and prophets of old.

With your own hand send down into this oil the power of the Holy Spirit so that all who shall be anointed with it may be kept safe from diseases and healed of all sicknesses; and may every Satanic adversary be exterminated through its power; make it an unction of your own grace through the name and through the power of our Lord Jesus Christ and the Holy Spirit. Amen.

[Adapted from an ancient Alexandrian prayer found in
The Statutes of the Apostles]

After blessing the oil, proceed to each participant and anoint him or her on the head and/or on the hands. Be liberal when applying the oil, and encourage the anointed to rub the oil into their skin. You may anoint in silence or you may wish to pray spontaneously, asking God's strength and healing for each person. When all have been anointed, ask one of the participants to anoint you.

Allow for several minutes of silent prayer following the anointing.

Prayers of Petition or Thanksgiving:

The mystagogue should voice one or two prayers and then invite the spontaneous prayers of the others.

Closing Song:

See suggestions in Chapter 4.

REFRESHMENTS (15 minutes)

DIALOGUE (55 minutes)

1. What was your predominant feeling as you remembered these Lenten rites?
2. What specific action from those rites touched you the most? What did it "say" to you?
3. To some people, exorcisms seem out of place in our "modern" world? How do you feel about them?
4. Some churches today do not require the profession of a specific creed by their members. Yet the Roman Catholic Church continues to adhere to these ancient formulas of belief. How do you feel about that?
5. When you apply the scripture reading about the man who was born blind to today, whom or what do you see in the various roles:
   - the blind man?
   - the parents?
   - the religious leaders?
   - the neighbors?
6. Some scholars believe that John was saying in this story that Jesus himself is much like the pool of Siloam. Why do you think this might be so? (Remember, John tells us that Siloam means "sent" or "one who has been sent.")
7. The religious leaders threw out the man born blind (they "ejected" him). Do you think this might mean that they excommunicated him? Has anyone rejected you because you of your Christian beliefs or because you joined the Catholic Church?

CLOSING PRAYER (5 minutes)

You may wish to close with a spontaneous prayer or with an agreed-upon common prayer.

DISMISSAL

SESSION III:
LIGHT AND LIFE

SUGGESTED USE OF TIME

7:30   Prayer
8:00   Refreshments
8:15   Dialogue
9:25   Closing Prayer
9:30   Dismissal

Environment:

The room should be dimly lit as the participants arrive. As soon as everyone is seated and you are ready to begin, all lights should be turned off. Prayer begins in total darkness. A Christ-candle, large taper, or the parish paschal candle should be ready in a separate room. You may wish to have neophytes bring their baptismal candles from the Easter vigil or you may wish to provide them with small tapers or with votive lights that they can take home with them.

PRAYER (30 minutes)

Lucernarium (Light Service)

Begin in total darkness. Allow group to experience the darkness for some time (two minutes, perhaps).

The mystagogue or other minister (cantor) enters the room with the lighted large candle. At the entrance to the room, the candle is elevated and the minister chants: "Christ our Light [or Lumen Christi]," as in the Easter vigil service. Group responds: "Thanks be to God [or Deo gratias]." This is done three times, as in the vigil service of light, with the cantor intoning the third "Christ our light" after placing the candle where it will remain for the rest of the evening. Small candles are lighted after the first, second, and third intonations.

If possible, have a cantor sing the Exsultet, or another suitable hymn could be sung by all.

The Remembering:

Recall for the participants the Easter vigil service of the new fire and the paschal candle. Particular elements you may wish to bring to mind:

- Gathering in the darkened church
- The bonfire outside the church
- Lighting of the paschal candle
- The procession into the church with the lighted paschal candle
- The Exsultet
- The smell of incense and smoldering wicks (when the congregation's candles were extinguished)

Scripture Reading:

John 1:1–5, 9–10
      8:12, 28–29
      12:32, 35–36

Prayers of Petition or Thanksgiving:

The mystagogue should voice one or two prayers and then invite spontaneous prayers from others.

Ancient Prayer of the Lucernarium

Mystagogue: The Lord be with you.
All: And also with you.

Mystagogue: Let us give thanks to the Lord, our God.
All: It is right to give God thanks and praise.

Mystagogue: To God are due greatness and majesty and glory.

             We thank you, O God, through your servant Jesus Christ, our Lord, for enlightening us by showing us the incorruptible light.

The day is over and we have come to the fall of night. We have been gladdened by the light of day that you have created for our joy.

And now that we lack not light for the evening, we hymn your holiness and glory, through your only Son, Jesus Christ, our Lord, through whom is given to you, with him and the Holy Spirit, glory, power, and honor now and for ever and ever.

All: Amen!

Hymn:

See suggestions in Chapter 4.

REFRESHMENTS (15 minutes)

DIALOGUE (1 hour and 10 minutes)

1. What was your predominant memory of the Easter vigil service of the light? Why?
2. Did any one symbol or symbolic action from this portion of the Easter vigil strike you as particularly powerful? Some possible responses: light/darkness, paschal candle, fire, procession into dark church, glow in the church when candles were lit, singing of the Exsultet, incense. Which one? Why?
3. In the scripture reading Jesus claims to be the light. What do you suppose he meant by using that image?
4. The light is described as life in the scripture reading. How can light be life?
5. How is Jesus light for you?
6. Can you give an example of how Jesus or belief in Jesus has been light in your life?
7. Jesus said that when he is lifted up, he would draw all people to himself. One meaning of "being lifted up" is crucifixion. Do you think there might be other meanings? What might they be?
8. Do you think the church is generally seen by others as comprising "children of light." If yes, in what ways? If no, why not?

CLOSING PRAYER (5 minutes)

You may wish to close with a spontaneous prayer or with an agreed-upon common prayer.

DISMISSAL

SESSION IV:
WATER AND SPIRIT

SUGGESTED USE OF TIME

7:30	Prayer
8:00	Refreshments
8:15	Dialogue
9:25	Closing Prayer
9:30	Dismissal

Environment:

Have a pitcher of water and a large bowl as the centerpiece of your prayer area. Use the Christ-candle from the last session or have another large, handsome candle situated close to the pitcher and water.

PRAYER (30 minutes)

Opening Song:

See suggestions in Chapter 4.

Opening Prayer:

Spontaneous by mystagogue.

The Remembering:

Recall for participants the moment of baptism at the Easter vigil. Ask those present who were already baptized and were received into full communion at the vigil and others present who were baptized as adults to remember their own baptisms as well as the baptisms that

they witnessed at the Easter vigil. Particular elements that you may
wish to bring to mind:

- The water
- The flow of the water if a fountain or waterfall was present
- The feel of the water as it coursed over the person's head
- What it felt like to be immersed, if this was an experience of any
of the participants
- The symbolism of death and rebirth, of cleansing

Scripture Reading:

John 3:1–21

Ritual Action:

At the conclusion of the reading, wait in reflective silence for
several minutes. Then the mystagogue should rise, go to the pitcher
and bowl, and slowly pour the water into the bowl while pronouncing
this blessing:

We humbly ask you, great God of eternal majesty, that
through our Lord Jesus Christ, his word, his power, and his
wisdom, you may send down the Holy Spirit, the Spirit of
adoption, upon this water, so that in its use your children will
remember their baptisms when all sins were washed away
and when they died with the Lord Jesus and rose up with him
into new life as your daughters and sons.

We ask this of you, Father, through the same Jesus Christ,
your Son, who lives and reigns with you in the unity of the
Holy Spirit, through all ages of ages. Amen.
[Adapted from a prayer for the Blessing of the Font
from *The Ambrosian Manual,* a liturgical
book of the tenth century]

Invite participants to approach the bowl individually, take water,
and bless themselves with it in memory of their baptisms.

If possible, have music playing in the background or sing a hymn
during this time. Allow music/singing to continue for several minutes
after last person has blessed himself or herself.

Prayers of Petition or Thanksgiving:

The mystagogue should voice one or two prayers and then invite spontaneous prayers from others.

Closing Song:

See suggestions in Chapter 4.

REFRESHMENTS (15 minutes)

DIALOGUE (1 hour and 10 minutes)

1. Nicodemus just doesn't seem to understand Jesus' words about baptism. Did you ever wonder why it was so necessary for people to be baptized?
2. Nicodemus comes to Jesus "in the night." Why do you suppose he did that? Did you ever feel as though you were coming to Jesus in the night—sort of covering your bets in case you decided Christianity wasn't for you?
3. When did you decide to be baptized? What brought you to that decision?
4. What were you feeling at the moment of baptism? Right afterward?
5. If you were immersed, could you tell the group what that felt like? What did it mean to you?
6. The scripture for this session speaks again of Jesus as the light who has come into the world. Has the light of Jesus caused you to see things differently since your baptism? What things? In what ways are they different now? In what ways are you different now?
7. In this translation there is the phrase, "Whoever lives the truth comes out into the light." "Lives the truth" seems an unusual phrase? Do you think it has a different meaning than "speaks the truth"?

CLOSING PRAYER (5 minutes)

You may wish to close with a spontaneous prayer or with an agreed-upon common prayer.

DISMISSAL

SESSION V:
BREAD AND LIFE

SUGGESTED USE OF TIME

7:30   Prayer
8:15   Refreshments
8:30   Dialogue
9:25   Closing Prayer
9:30   Dismissal

Environment:

Arrange for your centerpiece a plate with bread (a freshly baked loaf, dinner rolls, pita, matzoth), a decanter of wine (or grape juice), one goblet, a candle, flowers.

PRAYER (45 minutes)

Opening Song:

See suggestions in Chapter 4.

Opening Prayer:

Spontaneous by the mystagogue.

The Remembering

For this session, participants are asked to make a spoken response to each part. After allowing a few moments of silence the mystagogue says: "We give thanks." To this all respond: "We remember."

Recall for participants the Church's memories of the last supper —a seder meal—how Jesus took bread and pronounced the *berakah* (blessing): "Blessed are you, O Lord our God, king of the universe, who brings forth bread from the earth. . . ." (Silence)

Mystagogue: We give thanks.
All: We remember.

How Jesus then told his followers to take the bread and to eat it—that this was his body. (Silence)

Mystagogue: We give thanks.
All: We remember.

How Jesus took a cup of wine and offered the blessing: "Blessed are you, O Lord our God, king of the universe, who gives us wine from the grapes. . . ." (Silence)

Mystagogue: We give thanks.
All: We remember.

Then how Jesus told them to drink of the cup that was his blood of the new covenant, blood that would be shed for all—and how Jesus told his followers to do these things in his memory. (Silence)

Mystagogue: We give thanks.
All: We remember.

Recall for the participants their first communion—at the last Easter vigil or many, many years ago—that very first time they became intimately united with the Lord in holy communion.
Ask the participants to try to recapture their feelings at that moment. (Silence)

Mystagogue: We give thanks.
All: We remember.

Scripture Reading:

John 6:34–38, 44, 47–69

Ritual Action:

(Instrumental music might be playing in the background)
The mystagogue takes the plate of bread, breaks the bread into sufficient pieces for the group, and passes the plate to the nearest person, saying: "We remember." Each person, upon taking a piece of bread, says: "We remember."

All consume the bread.

After everyone has eaten his or her piece of bread, the mystagogue pours wine from the decanter into the goblet. The mystagogue lifts the goblet as for a toast and says: "Lord Jesus, to whom should we go? You have the words of eternal life . . . and we remember."

The mystagogue passes the goblet to the person next to her or him. That person raises the goblet in a toast and says: "We remember." Then each one passes the goblet to the next person who also offers the toast.

Allow several minutes of reflective silence with or without background music.

Prayers of Petition or Thanksgiving:

The mystagogue should voice one or two prayers and then invite spontaneous prayers from others.

Closing Song:

See suggestions in Chapter 4.

REFRESHMENTS (15 minutes)

You may wish to serve "bread snacks"—crackers, matzoth, etc. —with cheese. And more wine. But of course!

DIALOGUE (45 minutes)

1. Can you describe your feelings the first time you shared in communion at the table of the eucharist?
2. In what ways is the mass important to you?
3. The fathers of the church—those early bishops and teachers of the first seven centuries—had a very literal understanding of the bread

and wine of the eucharist being the body and blood of Christ. That understanding was based upon the parts of the gospel of John we read at this session and on the accounts of the last supper in Matthew, Mark, and Luke. How do you understand the presence of Jesus in the eucharist?

4. What do you think Jesus felt like when "many of his disciples went away and accompanied him no more"?
5. Have you ever been so upset with the church that you thought you ought to leave, but found that you were with Peter: "Lord, to whom shall we go?" Would you be able to tell the group about that experience?
6. Jesus described himself as "the light of the world" and he said that that light was life. In this session's scripture reading, Jesus calls himself "the bread of life" and "the living bread." What is he trying to tell us?
7. What implications does sharing in the eucharist have in your day-to-day life?

CLOSING PRAYER (15 minutes)

You may wish to close with a spontaneous prayer or with a common prayer of the group's choosing.

More Refreshments:

The celebration continues!

DISMISSAL

SESSION VI:
LOVE AND COMMITMENT

SUGGESTED USE OF TIME

7:30   Prayer
8:00   Refreshments
8:15   Dialogue
9:25   Closing Prayer
9:30   Dismissal

Environment:

Go to your attic (basement, garage, closet) and retrieve some shepherds and a sheep or two from your Christmas crèche (or borrow them from the parish). Arrange these figures as your centerpiece. Avoid the temptation to add evergreen boughs; instead, place cut flowers in vases and arrange green plants around the shepherds and sheep.

PRAYER (30 minutes)

Opening Song:

See suggestions in Chapter 4.

Opening Prayer:

Spontaneous by the mystagogue.

The Remembering:

Recall for participants one of the scrutinies or the giving over of the Lord's Prayer.
Particular elements you may wish to bring to mind:

Scrutinies:
 ■ The kneeling (bowing) during the prayer
 ■ The difficult things in my life that the Lord and the community were bringing into the light
 ■ The questions and doubts that I had as I searched and searched
 ■ The time I almost told Father or the catechumenate director or my sponsor that I was going to quit because I just could not give up: _____(ask group members to silently fill in this blank for themselves)

Giving of/Receiving the Lord's Prayer
 ■ The presentation of the church's "table prayer," the Lord's Prayer. How beautiful it was to *really* listen to the words as we prayed it together so slowly
 ■ How enthusiastically I can pray that God's kingdom will come
 ■ How difficult it is sometimes to say "thy will be done"
 ■ How eagerly I ask for forgiveness for my trespasses
 ■ How hard it is for me to forgive the people who have hurt me—especially people in my family or in the church

Scripture Reading:

John 21:14–22 (You may wish to use Psalm 23 as a spoken or sung response to this reading.)

Prayers of Petition or Thanksgiving:

The mystagogue should voice one or two prayers and then invite the spontaneous prayers of others.

Closing Song:

See suggestions in Chapter 4.

REFRESHMENTS (15 minutes)

DIALOGUE (1 hour and 10 minutes)

1. Why is Jesus always asking difficult questions?
2. Were you ever uncomfortable during the scrutinies? Can you tell the group about that?

3. Poor Peter. How do you think he felt during his "scrutiny" by the Lord?

4. What do you think Jesus meant when he told Peter to feed his lambs, look after his sheep, and feed his sheep? Is this a message for the pope and bishops, or do you think that Jesus might have been talking to all Christians?

5. When Peter became curious about (and maybe a bit jealous of) the beloved disciple, Jesus rather bluntly told him: "What's it to you? You are to follow me." What does that say to you for the living of day-to-day life?

6. It's easy to say, "Jesus, I love you." Why is it so difficult to follow through with the action which that love implies?

7. Do you believe that Jesus expects you to feed the lambs and tend the sheep? If so, how do you intend to do that?

CLOSING PRAYER (5 minutes)

You may wish to close with a spontaneous prayer or with a common prayer of the group.

DISMISSAL

SESSION VII:
POWER AND PEACE

SUGGESTED USE OF TIME

7:30	Prayer
8:00	Refreshments
8:15	Dialogue
9:25	Closing Prayer
9:30	Dismissal

Environment:

If possible, have a menorah (a seven-branched candelabrum) or have seven separate candlesticks as the dominant part of your prayer space. Have the candles unlighted as the session begins. Display the urn of oil that you used in the anointing rite during Cenacle Session II. Use plenty of flowers in your centerpiece arrangement.

PRAYER (30 minutes)

Opening Song:

See suggestions in Chapter 4.

Opening Prayer:

Spontaneous by the mystagogue.

Ritual Action:

Turn off all lights.
The mystagogue (or another) strikes a match and says:

"Come, Holy Spirit, bring us peace." (The group repeats the mystagogue's prayer.)

The mystagogue lights one candle and says:
"Come, Holy Spirit, bring us wisdom."
                    (Group repeats)

The mystagogue lights each candle in succession in the same way, with the group repeating each invocation:

"Come, Holy Spirit, bring us understanding."
"Come, Holy Spirit, bring us good counsel."
"Come, Holy Spirit, fill us with strength."
"Come, Holy Spirit, bring us knowledge."
"Come, Holy Spirit, bring us true piety."
"Come, Holy Spirit, help us stand in awe of the Lord.

The Remembering:

Recall for the participants the rite of confirmation. Particular elements that you might wish to mention:
- The prayer over you, when the presider stretched out his hands and asked that the Holy Spirit might descend upon you
- The words of the presider: "Be sealed with the gift of the Holy Spirit. . . . Peace be with you"
- The holy chrism—did you smell the balsam fragrance?
- The feel of the anointing itself
- How the oil is absorbed by the skin and becomes a part of you
- How the oil sticks to you

Scripture Reading:

John 20:19–22

Prayers of Petition or Thanksgiving:

The mystagogue should voice one or two prayers and then invite others to pray spontaneously.

Closing Song:

See suggestions in Chapter 4.

REFRESHMENTS (15 minutes)

DIALOGUE (1 hour and 10 minutes)

1. Did you have any strong feelings that you remembered about your confirmation?
2. How do you think your confirmation has helped/will help you live out your life as a Catholic Christian?
3. Does it strike you as strange that, in this scripture passage, the disciples did not seem to recognize Jesus at first? Why do you suppose that was?
4. When the disciples finally recognized Jesus, what caused them to do so?
5. What did the Father send Jesus to do?
6. Did Jesus ever receive the Holy Spirit?
7. What did Jesus send the disciples to do?
8. Does Jesus send us to do something? What?
9. Why do we need the Holy Spirit to carry out our mission?
10. How might that Spirit help us?
11. What do you think might be some very ordinary, everyday ways in which you can be an apostle (one who is sent) of Jesus today?

CLOSING PRAYER (5 minutes)

You may wish to close with spontaneous prayer or with a group common prayer.

DISMISSAL

6. General Background on the Gospel of John

We wish to emphasize once again that *Cenacle Sessions* is *not* meant to be a Bible study. Mystagogues should resist every temptation of their own and every effort of participants to transform this mystagogy into an academic exercise or into something that it is not intended to be. There is certainly a need for concentrated, guided, academically grounded scripture study within the Catholic community. Such study is encouraged. But such study is not the purpose of *Cenacle Sessions.* Therefore, comments here regarding the gospel of John will necessarily be brief.

These comments and notes are intended to give the mystagogue a general knowledge of the fourth gospel. They also attempt to anticipate questions about the scripture that might arise among participants during the sessions. Additionally, they are meant to be a means that will enable the mystagogue to enhance the meditation on the scriptural passages as a way of enriching the overriding purpose of *Cenacle Sessions:* facilitating the "savoring" experience.

Overview

Author

Authorship of the fourth gospel has traditionally been credited to John, one of the twelve, a Galilean fisherman, son of Zebedee and brother of James. This tradition dates as far back as the second century to Irenaeus (ca. A.D. 180). The state of scholarship and the information available at this time make this the best conclusion regarding authorship.

Biblical scholars have advanced many other theories regarding the identity of the author of the fourth gospel. These include:

- John the elder (or presbyter)
- John Mark (the companion of Barnabas and Paul in the Acts of the Apostles)

- the beloved disciple (for those who believe that John and the beloved disciple are two different persons)
- Lazarus (who some scholars believe was the beloved disciple)

Purpose

Scholars have identified several purposes of this gospel; each purpose has its own adherents. The choice of this gospel as a mystagogic vehicle for *Cenacle Sessions* is predicated on the fact that at least one of those purposes was to confirm the brothers and sisters in the faith. John wrote the gospel to assure the believers of the late first century that Jesus continued to be present to them in the community of faith —that Jesus was present even though the last of the eyewitnesses were dying and even though Jesus had not yet returned in glory.

John, concerned at the shakiness of faith manifest in his new sisters and brothers in the church, set himself about the task of writing an account of his Lord that would not only light a fire in their hearts but would also furnish them with food for meditation—food to nourish them and to bring them to a mature and solid faith.

The author of the fourth gospel himself states that the purpose of his writing the gospel account was "so that you may [come to] believe that Jesus is the messiah, the Son of God, and that through this belief you may have life in his name" (Jn 20:31).

While there is discussion among scholars as to the proper rendering of the verb *believe* in this verse (if in the present: "you may believe"; or if in the aorist, then: "you may come to believe"), it is generally agreed that John has structured the gospel to serve as a series of catechetical meditations on the sign (the sacrament) that is Jesus himself.

Date

Most contemporary scripture scholars date the gospel as early as A.D. 90 and not much later than A.D. 100. This runs counter to earlier beliefs that set the date of composition much later.

Today many scholars also agree that the fourth gospel reflects a tradition as ancient as (though different from) the tradition upon which the synoptic gospels of Matthew, Mark, and Luke are founded.

Place

Tradition sets the place of composition at Ephesus in Asia Minor. This belief is based upon other traditions that identify the apostle John as "bishop" of Ephesus. Many contemporary scholars, notably Raymond E. Brown, S.S., are now saying that the gospel was written in Palestine, or at least that it was composed out of the experiences of a Palestinian Jewish Christian community led by the beloved disciple.

Liturgical Influences/Sacramentality in the Gospel

There is sharp division among scripture scholars regarding the sacramentality found in John. The disagreements hinge on whether the evangelist was or was not catechizing his readers about the sacraments as found in the first century church and retrojecting sacramental practices into the life of Jesus.

There is little disagreement, however, that the gospel according to John is greatly influenced by the Jewish liturgy and that the author of the gospel paints a powerful picture of a life of Jesus infused with sacramentality. This is a subsidiary reason for choosing the fourth gospel as a mystagogic vehicle. The sacramental overtones in the various selections from this gospel ideally lend themselves to "The Remembering" of the rites of initiation.

While many Catholic scholars have seen a sacramentalism in John that is, perhaps, too broad, the vast majority of scholars cannot deny that strong baptismal and eucharistic images are found in the gospel. Raymond E. Brown, in his *Anchor Bible* commentary, states that "by associating baptism and the eucharist with Jesus' own words and actions, John is once more trying to show the roots of church life in Jesus himself" (Vol. 29, p. cxi) and "the gospel's intention [is] to show how the institutions of the Christian life are rooted in what Jesus said and did in his life" (p. cxiv).

Cenacle Sessions urges mystagogues to do the same.

The "I Am" Statements of Jesus

The fourth gospel contains at least twenty-one instances in which Jesus refers to himself with the words *I am* (a list of these follows). Four of the seven scripture selections used in *Cenacle Sessions* contain instances of this usage:

Session I:
- I am the true vine (15:1)
- I am the vine (15:5)

Session II:
- I am the light of the world (9:5)

Session III:
- I am the light of the world (8:12)
- When you lift up the Son of Man, then you will realize that I AM (8:28)

Session V:
- I am the bread of life (6:35 and 6:47)
- I am the living bread (6:51)

In five of the statements, the "I am" is used absolutely, and there is little doubt that John wishes to portray Jesus as having used the divine name (YHWH = I AM WHO I AM, I AM THE EXISTING ONE). One of these absolute usages occurs during *Cenacle Sessions* (in Session III: "When you lift up the Son of Man, then you will realize that I AM.")

In the other instances of the "I am" in John, each occurs with an obvious or an understood predicate nominative; in these cases, the "I am" is to be understood by the reader as a figurative usage ("I am the light of the world," "I am the true vine," "I am the bread of life," etc.). This use in John is analogous to the use of parables in the synoptic gospels.

Raymond Brown believes that the absolute use of the "I am" in John forms the basis for the other, figurative uses. All uses, however, seem to be meant to bring to the reader's mind the idea of the divine name found in the Hebrew scriptures.

USE OF I AM (ἐγώ εἰμι) IN JOHN'S GOSPEL

†6:20: It is I. Do not be afraid.

♦6:35, 47, 51: I am the bread of life; I am the living bread.

♦8:12; 9:5: I am the light of the world.

8:18: I testify on my behalf. [I am one who gives testimony on my behalf.]

8:23: I am from above. [I belong to what is above.]

*8:24: For, if you do not believe that I AM [he], you will die in your sins.

*8:28: When you lift up the Son of Man, then you will realize that I AM.

*8:58: Before Abraham came to be, I AM.

♦10:7, 9: I am the gate for the sheep; I am the gate.

♦10:11, 14: I am the good shepherd.

♦11:25: I am the resurrection and the life.

*13:19: When it happens, you may believe that I AM.

♦14:6: I am the way and the truth and the life.

♦15:1, 5: I am the true vine; I am the vine.

†18:5: I am [he] (at his arrest in the garden).

---

† predicate understood
♦with a predicate nominative (figuratively)
* absolute

7. Notes on Individual Gospel Selections

Session I: Called and Chosen—John 15:1–17

This passage of the gospel deals with the relationship of the individual Christian to Jesus and to the Christian community.

One of John's purposes in his gospel is to show that Jesus is the source of life—new life now and everlasting life after death. The image of the vine reinforces this purpose. Please note that Jesus is the entire vine (not just the central stalk); therefore, the branches are part of the vine, i.e., the individual Christian is actually part of Jesus, not merely a branch that has been grafted onto him. This image is close to that of the Pauline image of the church as the body of Christ.

The image of the vine and branches is an image from the Jewish scriptures. The vineyard and the vine are images of Israel in the Old Testament. In Ezekiel 17, the vine is the Davidic king. Wisdom is also personified as a vine (see Sir 24:17–21, for instance).

Here, in vv. 1 and 5, is the use of the I AM statement. It is interesting to note that the Greek word for branches used in this passage (v. 5 et al.) is *klémata,* which means *grapevines* or *vines.* It is also the word that botanists have used to name the popular flowering vine, the clematis. If you have a clematis vine that happens to be in bloom at the time this session is held, you may wish to use its blossoms in the centerpiece for this session.

The vine is seen by some scholars as a eucharistic image because the branches feed on and drink from the vine.

The verses where Jesus called his followers *friends* formed the basis for the Quakers' naming themselves the Society of Friends.

At the root of the English word *friend* is the connotation of *free* or *freedom,* an indication that real friends allow one to be free, to be authentically oneself.

Those who are called and chosen (elected) are also to be sent forth to bear fruit. John may wish to show here that the eleven are to be model Christians for the rest of us and that we are each called, chosen, and sent forth to bear fruit.

"Love one another." The tense and mood of the Greek verb suggests a love that is continuous and lifelong.

Session II: Sight and Insight—John 9:1–41

Many scholars call this the most brilliant passage in the entire gospel.

The cure of the man born blind is one of the "signs" in the gospel of John. It is meant to signify the triumph of light over darkness; the gift of physical sight signifies the gift of the sight of faith.

This gospel story also reflects the tension that existed between the synagogue and the church in John's time. "The Jews" in John's gospel invariably refers on one level to the Jerusalem authorities at the time of Jesus and on another level to the Judaism of the 90s. It was at that time that the disciples of Moses excommunicated the Jewish disciples of Jesus from the synagogues. Is the blind man on trial a type for those Christian Jews who were called upon in the 90s to publicly confess their belief in Jesus—a confession that would result in their disinheritance from Israel and their excommunication from the synagogue?

The story of the man born blind is a baptismal lesson, and during the patristic period it served as a reading for the rite of the great scrutiny. When the lector arrived at verse 38 ("He [the blind man] said, 'I do believe, Lord' and he worshiped him"), the reading stopped and the elect then rendered the creed to the bishop and the community.

Jesus' use of spittle also became part of the church's baptismal ceremony for many centuries because of this gospel story. The verb describing Jesus' action of applying the spittle-mud paste is rendered *smeared* in this translation; however, it is the same Greek word that is often translated *anointed.* This is the reason that an anointing ceremony is suggested for this session; this is why you are asked to recall for the neophytes the anointing and the scrutinies they experienced during the catechumenal period and during Lent.

The name of the pool—Siloam—means "one who has been sent" (or, as the NAB revised New Testament has it, "sent"). Some scholars maintain that John wished his readers to understand that Jesus (the one who had been sent by the Father) was like the pool—a source of healing, light, sight (both physical and spiritual), and new life. We are baptized into Christ who washes us clean with his blood and gives us new sight.

The parents in the story may be types for those Christians from John's community who wavered in their belief when confronted by the Jewish authorities. The parents are those Jewish Christians who (in A.D. 90) found themselves in the dilemma of renouncing either Judaism or Jesus.

Session III: Light and Life—
John 1:1-5, 9-10; 8:12, 28-29; 12:32, 35-36

The first part of the reading is taken from the so-called prologue to the gospel, which is thought to have been an independent hymn used in the liturgy. Note that the beginning of John's gospel echoes the words of Genesis: "In the beginning. . . ."

Light and darkness is a major, recurring theme in John's gospel. Jesus was the real, but by-and-large unrecognized, light. Those who refused to recognize him were those who chose to remain in the darkness.

Elsewhere in the gospel, Jesus refers to himself as life-giving bread and as water that is life-giving. Here it is life-giving light. While we do not usually think of light as living, it is certainly true that light is a source of life itself. Without the sun there would be no photosynthesis, no vegetation, no food, no life—human or otherwise. So in a very real sense, light is life.

On the spiritual level, Jesus is light; Jesus is the source of life; Jesus is the sun of Justice; Jesus is the light that is reflected in believers.

The incident in the passage from chapter 8 occurs during the Jewish autumnal harvest feast of Tabernacles (Booths, Tents, Huts [*Sukkôt*]), where great fires were lighted in four candlesticks in the Court of the Women in the temple precincts. This is the scene, then, as Jesus shouts to the assembled worshipers: "I am the light of the world. (These great lights in this temple court are not the lights. I am the light of the world.")

The "lifting up" of Jesus occurs several times throughout the gospel: in the Nicodemus story, at the scene during the feast of Tabernacles, and at the theophany when Jesus enters Jerusalem in triumph. The "lifting up" hearkens back to Moses' lifting up the bronze serpent in the desert in a healing ritual; it looks forward to Jesus' crucifixion, resurrection, and ascension; it also contains the image or connotation of the exaltation of Jesus by Christians as Lord and messiah.

In John 8:28 we have one instance of the absolute use of an "I AM" statement: "When you lift up the Son of Man, then you will realize that I AM."

"Children of the light" was another title the Quakers used to refer to themselves before they settled on the "Society of Friends" (see notes for Session I).

Session IV: Water and Spirit—John 3:1–21

Nicodemus is cast in the role of the sincere religious seeker whose questioning allows Jesus the opportunity to expound his teaching. Nicodemus has been drawn to Jesus by the signs that Jesus performed.

Jesus obviously believes Nicodemus is sincere and is interested in the truth: he begins three mini-discourses in this short passage with "Amen, amen, I say to you. . . ." This phrase could have been translated: Truly, truly, I tell you . . . or In all truth I tell you.

This passage illustrates a common device of John: to have Jesus speak on one level while those he has engaged (or who have engaged him) in dialogue think and respond on another level. A useful literary device, certainly, but how true to life! How often have you heard the phrase (well past becoming a cliché): "What we have here is a communications problem!"

Nicodemus may have come to Jesus "in the night" not out of fear of being recognized in daylight, but simply because it was a custom of the rabbis to study the scriptures at night. On the other hand, the image of Nicodemus "being in the dark" should not be lost on readers.

Nicodemus appears next in chapter 7, where, although he is not yet a follower of Jesus, he speaks in Jesus' behalf. His final appearance is with Joseph of Arimathea at Jesus' burial, where he seems to be portrayed as one who has become a believer. Perhaps Nicodemus is a model for neophytes. They, like him, have come to know Jesus over time; they, like him, questioned; they, like him, came from ignorance to knowledge, from confusion to understanding, from darkness to light.

Session V: Bread and Life—John 6:34–38, 44, 47–69

The event in this passage takes place following the multiplication of five barley loaves and two fish to feed at least five thousand men.

This is an obvious eucharistic discourse. It is interesting to note that John tells us that "Jesus took the loaves, gave thanks, and distributed them. . . ." The Greek word for giving thanks is *eucharistésas,* hence eucharist.

We have again in this passage John's device of having Jesus speak on one level while being misunderstood by his hearers who are operating on another level. (See notes on Session IV.)

Notice that the same questions about the living bread here were asked by the Samaritan woman about the living water. Note also that this living bread will completely satisfy those who eat it as the living water would completely satisfy those who drank it.

The poignancy of the scene where Jesus is rejected by many of his followers should offer much food for thought and discussion.

Some scholars believe that Peter's profession in vv. 68–69 is John's version of the tradition found in Matthew 16. Peter, like the neophytes, has taken the risk and has thrown their lot with the Lord.

Session VI: Love and Commitment—John 21:14–22

This passage is taken from the final chapter of the gospel, which is regarded as an addition to the original version. It is found in every ancient manuscript of John still in existence, so it must have been added extremely early. It is believed to have been added by one of the disciples of the gospel's author.

This scene is magnificent material for a meditation on reconciliation: how Jesus so readily accepts us back after we have denied him. Here, as one commentator has observed, the breakfast fire on the beach serves as a literary link to the charcoal fire in the high priest's courtyard where Peter denied Jesus. Peter is given the opportunity to profess his love for Jesus, and he is given the opportunity to do so three times—each time wiping out one of the three denials.

Most commentators see no great significance in the slight differences in Jesus' commands to Peter. "Feed my lambs . . . tend my sheep . . . feed my sheep . . ." all represent the same mandate to shepherd the community.

A rumor regarding the beloved disciple (John?) is dealt with in this passage. Word had it that the beloved disciple would not die before the Lord returned. Apparently, at the time of the writing of this portion of the gospel, the beloved disciple had died; hence, we have one of the reasons this epilogue was appended by one of the disciples of the beloved disciple.

Of note is Jesus' rather terse reply to the curious Peter who asks Jesus (about the beloved disciple): "Lord, what about him?" Jesus more or less suggests that Peter (and all the other Christians in John's community who are upset and confused over the death of the one-who-wasn't-supposed-to-die-until-the-Lord's-return) should perhaps tend to the business of following him. This might be a wonderful discussion topic for the neophytes: When it all gets boiled down, this is what we are about—following Jesus.

Session VII: Power and Peace—John 20:19–22

This scene takes place in the cenacle on the evening of Easter day.

Note that the disciples did not recognize Jesus immediately. In fact, they did not recognize Jesus until "he showed them his hands and his side." It could be said that the wounds of Jesus are the ultimate sign of his ministry to us. He loved us so much that he gave his all, he laid down his life, for us. And his wounds serve as the sign, the certification, the proof, of that love.

As Christians, will others see Jesus in us because of our wounds? Have we laid down our lives sufficiently that our identification with Jesus is evident from our ministry?

Jesus sends us forth ("apostles" us) in the power of the Spirit of peace. Is he sending us forth to be wounded?

Even the disciples didn't recognize Jesus just because he came among them wishing them peace. Do we expect people to see Jesus in us just because we offer them words of peace? Or is more being asked of us?

8. Scripture Texts Used in the Sessions

Session I: Called and Chosen—John 15:1–17

[At the Last Supper, Jesus told his disciples:]

"I am the true vine, and my Father is the vine grower. He takes away every branch in me that does not bear fruit, and everyone that does he prunes so that it bears more fruit. You are already pruned because of the word that I spoke to you. Remain in me, as I remain in you. Just as a branch cannot bear fruit on its own unless it remains on the vine, so neither can you unless you remain in me. I am the vine, you are the branches. Whoever remains in me and I in him will bear much fruit, because without me you can do nothing. Anyone who does not remain in me will be thrown out like a branch and wither; people will gather them and throw them into a fire and they will be burned. If you remain in me and my words remain in you, ask for whatever you want and it will be done for you. By this is my Father glorified, that you bear much fruit and become my disciples. As the Father loves me, so I also love you. Remain in my love. If you keep my commandments, you will remain in my love, just as I have kept my Father's commandments and remain in his love.

"I have told you this so that my joy might be in you and your joy might be complete. This is my commandment: love one another as I love you. No one has greater love than this, to lay down one's life for one's friends. You are my friends if you do what I command you. I no longer call you slaves, because a slave does not know what his master is doing. I have called you friends, because I have told you everything I have heard from my Father. It was not you who chose me, but I who chose you and appointed you to go and bear fruit that will remain, so that whatever you ask the Father in my name he may give you. This I command you: love one another."

Session II: Sight and Insight—John 9:1–41

As [Jesus] passed by he saw a man blind from birth. His disciples asked him, "Rabbi, who sinned, this man or his parents, that he was born blind?" Jesus answered, "Neither he nor his parents sinned; it is so that the works of God might be made visible through him. We have to do the works of the one who sent me while it is day. Night is coming when no one can work. While I am in the world, I am the light of the world." When he had said this, he spat on the ground and made clay with the saliva, and smeared the clay on his eyes, and said to him, "Go wash in the Pool of Siloam" (which means Sent). So he went and washed, and came back able to see.

His neighbors and those who had seen him earlier as a beggar said, "Isn't this the one who used to sit and beg?" Some said, "It is," but others said, "No, he just looks like him." He said, "I am." So they said to him, "[So] how were your eyes opened?" He replied, "The man called Jesus made clay and anointed my eyes and told me, 'Go to Siloam and wash.' So I went there and washed and was able to see." And they said to him, "Where is he?" He said, "I don't know."

They brought the one who was once blind to the Pharisees. Now Jesus had made clay and opened his eyes on a sabbath. So then the Pharisees also asked him how he was able to see. He said to them, "He put clay on my eyes, and I washed, and now I can see." So some of the Pharisees said, "This man is not from God, because he does not keep the sabbath." [But] others said, "How can a sinful man do such signs?" And there was a division among them.

So they said to the blind man again, "What do you have to say about him, since he opened your eyes?" He said, "He is a prophet."

Now the Jews did not believe that he had been blind and gained his sight until they summoned the parents of the one who had gained his sight. They asked them, "Is this your son, who you say was born blind? How does he now see?" His parents answered and said, "We know that this is our son and that he was born blind. We do not know how he sees now, nor do we know who opened his eyes. Ask him, he is of age; he can speak for himself."

His parents said this because they were afraid of the Jews, for the Jews had already agreed that if anyone acknowledged him as the Messiah, he would be expelled from the synagogue. For this reason his parents said, "He is of age; question him."

So a second time they called the man who had been blind and said to him, "Give God the praise! We know that this man is a sinner." He replied, "If he is a sinner, I do not know. One thing I do know is that I was blind and now I see." So they said to him, "What did he do to you? How did he open your eyes?" He answered them, "I told you already and you did not listen. Why do you want to hear it again? Do you want to become his disciples, too?" They ridiculed him and said, "You are that man's disciple; we are disciples of Moses! We know that God spoke to Moses, but we do not know where this one is from." The man answered and said to them, "This is what is so amazing, that you do not know where he is from, yet he opened my eyes. We know that God does not listen to sinners, but if one is devout and does his will, he listens to him. It is unheard of that anyone ever opened the eyes of a person born blind. If this man were not from God, he would not be able to do anything." They answered and said to him, "You were born totally in sin, and are you trying to teach us?" Then they threw him out.

When Jesus heard that they had thrown him out, he found him and said, "Do you believe in the Son of Man?" He answered and said, "Who is he, sir, that I may believe in him?" Jesus said to him, "You have seen him and the one speaking with you is he." He said, "I do believe, Lord," and he worshiped him.

Then Jesus said, "I came into this world for judgment, so that those who do not see might see, and those who do see might become blind."

Some of the Pharisees who were with him heard this and said to him, "Surely we are not also blind, are we?" Jesus said to them, "If you were blind, you would have no sin; but now you are saying, 'We see,' so your sin remains."

Session III: Light and Life—
John 1:1–5, 9–10; 8:12, 28–29; 12:32, 35–36

In the beginning was the Word,
  and the Word was with God,
  and the Word was God.
He was in the beginning with God.
  All things came to be through him,
  and without him nothing came to be.
What came to be through him was life,
  and this life was the light of the human race;
  the light shines in the darkness,
  and the darkness has not overcome it.

* * *

The true light, which enlightens everyone, was coming into the world.

He was in the world,
   and the world came to be through him,
   but the world did not know him.

* * *

Jesus spoke to them again, saying, "I am the light of the world. Whoever follows me will not walk in darkness, but will have the light of life."

So Jesus said [to them], "When you lift up the Son of Man, then you will realize that I AM, and that I do nothing on my own, but I say only what the Father taught me. The one who sent me is with me. He has not left me alone, because I always do what is pleasing to him."

* * *

[Jesus said:] "And when I am lifted up from the earth, I will draw everyone to myself."

Jesus said to them, "The light will be among you only a little while. Walk while you have the light, so that darkness may not overcome you. Whoever walks in the dark does not know where he is going. While you have the light, believe in the light, so that you may become children of the light."

Session IV: Water and Spirit—John 3:1–21

Now there was a Pharisee named Nicodemus, a ruler of the Jews. He came to Jesus at night and said to him, "Rabbi, we know that you are a teacher who has come from God, for no one can do these signs that you are doing unless God is with him." Jesus answered and said to him, "Amen, amen, I say to you, no one can see the kingdom of God without being born from above." Nicodemus said to him, "How can a person once grown old be born again? Surely he cannot reenter his mother's womb and be born again, can he?" Jesus answered, "Amen,

amen, I say to you, no one can enter the kingdom of God without being born of water and Spirit. What is born of flesh is flesh and what is born of spirit is spirit. Do not be amazed that I told you, 'You must be born from above.' The wind blows where it wills, and you can hear the sound it makes, but you do not know where it comes from or where it goes; so it is with everyone who is born of the Spirit."

Nicodemus answered and said to him, "How can this happen?" Jesus answered and said to him, "You are the teacher of Israel and you do not understand this? Amen, amen, I say to you, we speak of what we know and we testify to what we have seen, but you people do not accept our testimony. If I tell you about earthly things and you do not believe, how will you believe if I tell you about heavenly things? No one has gone up to heaven except the one who has come down from heaven, the Son of Man. And just as Moses lifted up the serpent in the desert, so must the Son of Man be lifted up so that everyone who believes in him may have eternal life.

For God so loved the world that he gave his only Son, so that everyone who believes in him might not perish but might have eternal life.

For God did not send his Son into the world to condemn the world, but that the world might be saved through him. Whoever believes in him will not be condemned, but whoever does not believe has already been condemned, because he has not believed in the name of the only Son of God. And this is the verdict, that the light came into the world, but people preferred darkness to light, because their works were evil. For everyone who does wicked things hates the light and does not come toward the light, so that his works might not be exposed. But whoever lives the truth comes to the light, so that his works may be clearly seen as done in God.

Session V: Bread and Life—John 6:35–38, 44, 47–69

Jesus said to them, "I am the bread of life; whoever comes to me will never hunger and whoever believes in me will never thirst. But I told you that although you have seen [me], you do not believe. Everything that the Father gives me will come to me, and I will not reject anyone who comes to me, because I came down from heaven not to do my own will but the will of the one who sent me.

*   *   *

"No one can come to me unless the Father who sent me draw him, and I will raise him on the last day.

* * *

"Amen, amen, I say to you, whoever believes has eternal life. I am the bread of life. Your ancestors ate the manna in the desert, but they died; this is the bread that comes down from heaven so that one may eat it and not die. I am the living bread that comes down from heaven; whoever eats this bread will live forever; and the bread that I will give is my flesh for the life of the world."

The Jews quarreled among themselves, saying, "How can this man give us [his] flesh to eat?" Jesus said to them, "Amen, amen, I say to you, unless you eat the flesh of the Son of Man and drink his blood, you do not have life within you. Whoever eats my flesh and drinks my blood has eternal life, and I will raise him on the last day. For my flesh is true food, and my blood is true drink. Whoever eats my flesh and drinks my blood remains in me and I in him. Just as the living Father sent me and I have life because of the Father, so also the one who feeds on me will have life because of me. This is the bread that came down from heaven. Unlike your ancestors who ate and still died, whoever eats this bread will live forever." These things he said while teaching in the synagogue in Capernaum.

Then many of his disciples who were listening said, "This saying is hard; who can accept it?" Since Jesus knew that his disciples were murmuring about this, he said to them, "Does this shock you? What if you were to see the Son of Man ascending to where he was before? It is the spirit that gives life, while the flesh is of no avail. The words I have spoken to you are spirit and life. But there are some of you who do not believe." Jesus knew from the beginning the ones who would not believe and the one who would betray him. And he said, "For this reason I have told you that no one can come to me unless it is granted him by my Father."

As a result of this, many [of] his disciples returned to their former way of life and no longer accompanied him. Jesus then said to the Twelve, "Do you also want to leave?" Simon Peter answered him, "Master, to whom shall we go? You have the words of eternal life. We have come to believe and are convinced that you are the Holy One of God."

Session VI: Love and Commitment—John 21:14–22

[After Jesus had been raised from the dead, he appeared to his disciples at dawn on the shore of the Sea of Tiberias where he fixed them a breakfast of bread and grilled fish.] This was now the third time Jesus was revealed to his disciples after being raised from the dead.

When they had finished breakfast, Jesus said to Simon Peter, "Simon, son of John, do you love me more than these?" He said to him, "Yes, Lord, you know that I love you." He said to him, "Feed my lambs." He then said to him a second time, "Simon, son of John, do you love me?" He said to him, "Yes, Lord, you know that I love you." He said to him, "Tend my sheep." He said to him the third time, "Simon, son of John, do you love me?" Peter was distressed that he had said to him a third time, "Do you love me?" and he said to him, "Lord, you know everything; you know that I love you." [Jesus] said to him, "Feed my sheep. Amen, amen, I say to you, when you were younger you used to dress yourself and go where you wanted; but when you grow old, you will stretch out your hands, and someone else will dress you and lead you where you do not want to go." He said this signifying by what kind of death he would glorify God. And when he had said this, he said to him, "Follow me."

Peter turned and saw the disciple following whom Jesus loved, the one who had also reclined upon his chest during the supper and had said, "Master, who is the one who will betray you?" When Peter saw him, he said to Jesus, "Lord, what about him?" Jesus said to him, "What if I want him to remain until I come? What concern is it of yours? You follow me."

Session VII: Power and Peace—John 20:19–22

On the evening of that first day of the week, when the doors were locked, where the disciples were, for fear of the Jews, Jesus came and stood in their midst and said to them, "Peace be with you."

When he had said this, he showed them his hands and his side. The disciples rejoiced when they saw the Lord. [Jesus] said to them again, "Peace be with you. As the Father has sent me, so I send you." And when he had said this, he breathed on them and said to them, "Receive the holy Spirit."

Bibliography

Anderson, William A. *Journeying Through the RCIA*. Dubuque: Wm. C. Brown Company Publishers, 1984.

Bacik, James J. *Apologetics and the Eclipse of Mystery: Mystagogy According to Karl Rahner*. Notre Dame: University of Notre Dame Press, 1980.

Baerwald, Jeffrey P., S.J. "Mystagogy: Structure, Content, Task," *The Chicago Catechumenate,* Volume 8, Number 4, May 1986, pp. 4–15.

Barr, Blaine G. "How Can a Large Parish Become a Viable Catechumenal Community," *Becoming a Catholic Christian.* (Advance Publication) New York: William H. Sadlier, Inc., 1978, pp. 49–53.

Bihlmeyer, Karl and Hermann Tüchle. *Church History.* [*Kirchengeschichte*] Volume I. Westminster: The Newman Press, 1968.

Bourgeois, Henri. "The Catechumenate in France Today," *Becoming a Catholic Christian.* (Advance Publication) New York: William H. Sadlier, Inc., 1978, pp. 20–34.

Bouyer, Louis. *The Spirituality of the New Testament and the Fathers.* New York: The Seabury Press, 1982.

Boyack, Kenneth, C.S.P. "Caring for New Catholics," *The Chicago Catechumenate.* Volume 7, Number 4, May 1985, pp. 4–12.

Bromiley, Geoffrey W. *Historical Theology: An Introduction.* Grand Rapids: Eerdmans, 1978.

Brown, Raymond E., S.S. *The Community of the Beloved Disciple.* New York: Paulist Press, 1979.

———. *The Gospel According to John,* Two Volumes. (*The Anchor Bible*) Garden City: Doubleday & Co., Inc., 1966.

———. *The Gospel of St. John, The Johannine Epistles.* (*New Testament Reading Guide*) Collegeville: The Liturgical Press, 1960.

———. "The Kerygma of the Gospel According to John," *Interpretation,* Volume 21, Number 4, October 1967, pp. 386–400.

Burtchaell, James Tunstead. "A New Pastoral Method in Theology," *Commonweal,* January 24, 1984, Volume III, Number 2, pp. 44–49.

Case, Shirley Jackson. *Makers of Christianity.* Port Washington: Kennikat Press, 1934, 1962, 1971.

Clark, Mary T. *Augustine of Hippo. (The Classics of Western Spirituality).* Ramsey: Paulist Press, 1984.

Clay, Michael. "Mystagogia and Catechesis on the Sacraments." *The Chicago Catechumenate.* Volume 6, Number 4, May 1984, pp. 11–16.

Cross, F.L., editor. *St. Cyril of Jerusalem's Lectures on the Christian Sacraments: The Procatechesis and the Five Mystagogical Lectures.* Crestwood: St. Vladimir's Seminary Press, 1977.

Duffey, Regis A., O.F.M. *On Becoming a Catholic.* San Francisco: Harper & Row, Publishers, 1984.

Duggan, Robert. "Mystagogy and Continual Conversion: RCIA Success Stories," *Christian Initiation Resources Reader,* Volume IV: *Mystagogia and Ministries.* New York: William H. Sadlier, Inc., 1984, pp. 19–30.

Dujarier, Michel. *A History of the Catechumenate: The First Six Centuries.* New York: William H. Sadlier, Inc., 1979.

Dunning, James B. *Ministries: Sharing God's Gifts.* Winona: Saint Mary's Press, 1985.

———. *New Wine: New Wineskins.* Chicago: William H. Sadlier, Inc., 1981.

———. "The Period of Mystagogia." *Christian Initiation Resources Reader,* Volume IV: *Mystagogia and Ministries.* New York: William H. Sadlier, Inc., 1984, pp. 7–18.

———. "The Stages of Initiation: Part IV. The Sacraments of Initiation and Afterwards," *Becoming a Catholic Christian.* (Advance Publication) New York: William H. Sadlier, Inc., 1978, pp. 123–131.

Dvornik, Francis. *The Ecumenical Councils.* Volume 82 of The Twentieth Century Encyclopedia of Catholicism. New York: Hawthorne Books, Inc., 1961.

"Eight Ages of Man." Summary paper on Erikson's Life Cycles, Adult Education Department, Indiana University/Purdue University at Indianapolis, ca. 1982.

Field, Anne, O.S.B. *From Darkness to Light.* Ann Arbor: Servant Books, 1978.

Finn, Edward E., S.J. *These Are My Rites.* Collegeville: The Liturgical Press, 1980.

Flanagan, Neal M., O.S.M. *The Gospel of St. John and the Johannine*

Epistles. (*Collegeville Bible Commentary*) Volume 4. Collegeville: The Liturgical Press, 1983.

Frend, W.H.C. *The Rise of Christianity.* Philadelphia: Fortress Press,
1984.

Gelineau, Joseph. "The Symbols of Christian Initiation," *Becoming a
Catholic Christian.* (Advance Publication) New York: William
H. Sadlier, Inc., 1978, pp. 178–184.

Gingras, George E. *Egeria: Diary of a Pilgrimage.* (Volume 38: *Ancient Christian Writers*) New York: Newman Press, 1970.

González, Justo L. *A History of Christian Thought.* Two Volumes.
Nashville: Abingdon, 1970.

Greer, Rowan A. *Origen.* (*The Classics of Western Spirituality*) New
York: Paulist Press, 1979.

Gregg, Robert C. *Athanasius.* (*The Classics of Western Spirituality*)
New York: Paulist Press, 1980.

Gusmer, Charles W. "Celebrating the Easter Season," *Christian Initiation Resources Reader.* Volume IV: *Mystagogia and Ministries,*
1984, pp. 31–39.

Guzie, Tad. "Theological Challenges," *Becoming a Catholic Christian.* (Advance Publication) New York: William H. Sadlier, Inc.,
1978, pp. 153–161.

Harkins, Paul W. *St. John Chrysostom: Baptismal Instructions.* (Volume 31: *Ancient Christian Writers*) Westminster: The Newman
Press, 1963.

———. *St. John Chrysostom: On the Incomprehensible Nature of God.*
(*The Fathers of the Church*) Washington, D.C.: The Catholic University of America, 1984.

Hart, Kevin T. "Adapting the Easter Vigil Service: Playing with Fire?"
Christian Initiation Resources Reader, Volume IV: *Mystagogia
and Ministries.* New York: William H. Sadlier, Inc., 1984, pp.
70–90.

Hunter, Archibald M. *According to John.* London: SCM Press Ltd.,
1968.

Jurgens, William A. *The Faith of the Early Fathers.* Three Volumes.
Collegeville: The Liturgical Press, 1979.

Kelly, J.N.D. *Early Christian Doctrines.* Second Edition. New York:
Harper & Row, Publishers, 1960.

Kemp, Raymond B. *A Journey in Faith.* New York: William H. Sadlier, Inc., 1979.

———. "Mystagogia: A Time To Be Fully Alive," *Christian Initiation
Resources.* New York: William H. Sadlier, Inc., Volume II, 1982.

———. "The Mystagogical Experience," *Christian Initiation Resources Reader,* Volume IV: *Mystagogia and Ministries.* New York: William H. Sadlier, Inc., 1984, pp. 54–69.

———. "The Mystagogical Principle in the Rite and in Catechesis," *Christian Initiation Resources.* New York: William H. Sadlier, Inc., Volume II, 1981.

Kennedy, Dennis, C.M. "The Lectionary as Content," *The Chicago Catechumenate,* Volume 8, Number 3, March 1986, pp. 13–17.

Kucharek, Casimir. *The Sacramental Mysteries: A Byzantine Approach.* Ontario: Alleluia Press, 1976.

Kysar, Robert. *John, the Maverick Gospel.* Richmond: John Knox Press, 1975.

Lawler, Thomas Comerford. *The Letters of St. Jerome.* Volume I. *(Ancient Christian Writers)* Westminster: Newman Press, 1963.

Lewinski, Ronald J. "Towards a Children's Catechumenate," *Christian Initiation Resources Reader,* Volume IV: *Mystagogia and Ministries.* New York: William H. Sadlier, Inc., 1984, pp. 100–111.

———. *Welcoming the New Catholic.* (Revised Edition) Chicago: Liturgy Training Publications, 1983.

Lopresti, James J. "Ritual and Conversion," *Christian Initiation Resources Reader,* Volume IV: *Mystagogia and Ministries.* New York: William H. Sadlier, Inc., 1984.

Martos, Joseph. *Doors to the Sacred: A Historical Introduction to Sacraments in the Catholic Church.* Garden City: Doubleday & Company, Inc., 1981.

Mitchell, Leonel L. *The Meaning of Ritual.* Ramsey: Paulist Press, 1977.

Nocent, Adrian, O.S.B. *The Liturgical Year.* Four Volumes. Collegeville: The Liturgical Press, 1977.

Pelikan, Jaroslav. *The Emergence of the Catholic Tradition (100–600),* Volume I *(The Christian Tradition).* Chicago: The University of Chicago Press, 1971.

Quasten, Johannes. *Patrology.* Three Volumes. Westminster: Christian Classics, Inc., 1983 (originally published 1960).

Radice, Betty, editor. *Early Christian Writings.* New York: Penguin Books, 1968.

Ramsey, Boniface, O.P. *Beginning To Read the Fathers.* New York: Paulist Press, 1985.

Randolph, Theresa, R.S.M. "Preliminary Survey on the Catechumenate in America Today," *Becoming a Catholic Christian.* (Advance Publication) New York: William H. Sadlier, Inc., 1978, pp. 35–38.

Rite of Christian Initiation of Adults. International Commission on English in the Liturgy, Inc. (ICEL), and the Bishops' Committee on the Liturgy of the National Conference of Catholic Bishops. Chicago: Liturgy Training Publications, 1988.

Rizzo, Cheryl. "The Experience of a Neophyte," *The Chicago Catechumenate,* Volume 6, Number 1, October 1983, pp. 27–28.

Reedy, William J., editor. *Becoming a Catholic Christian.* (Advance Publication Copy). New York: William H. Sadlier, Inc., 1978.

Relton, H. Maurice. *Studies in Christian Doctrine.* London: Macmillan & Co. Ltd., 1960.

Richardson, Alan. *Creeds in the Making.* Philadelphia: Fortress Press, 1981 (originally published: 1935).

Richardson, Cyril C., et al., editors. *Early Christian Fathers.* (Volume I: *The Library of Christian Classics*), Philadelphia: The Westminster Press, 1953.

Roberto, John. "RCIA: Implication for Youth Ministry," *Christian Initiation Resources Reader,* Volume IV: *Mystagogia and Ministries.* New York: William H. Sadlier, Inc., 1984, pp. 112–122.

Schaff, Philip, and Henry Wace, editors. *A Select Library of Nicene and Post-Nicene Fathers of the Christian Church.* Second Series. Volume VII: S. Cyril of Jerusalem and S. Gregory Nazianzen. Grand Rapids: Wm. B. Eerdmans Publishing Company, 1893.

Schnackenburg, Rudolf. *The Gospel According to John.* Volume I. New York: Herder and Herder, 1968. (Original edition: *Das Johannesevangelium,* Part I, Herder, Freiburg, 1965).

———. *The Gospel According to John.* Volume II. New York: The Seabury Press, 1980. (Original edition: *Das Johannesevangelium,* Part II, Verlag Herder KG, 1971).

Shea, John. "Using Scripture in Pastoral Settings," *Chicago Studies,* Volume 23, 1984, pp. 131–139.

Smith, D. Moody. "The Presentation of Jesus in the Fourth Gospel," *Interpretation,* Volume 31, 1977, pp. 367–378.

Sokol, Frank C. "The Rite of Christian Initiation and the Theology of the Church," *The Chicago Catechumenate,* Volume 8, Number 2, December 1985, pp. 5–12.

Stevenson, J., editor. *Creeds, Councils and Controversies.* London: S.P.C.K., 1972.

Stuhlmueller, Carroll, C.P. *Biblical Meditations for the Easter Season.* New York: Paulist Press, 1980.

Symbol: The Language of Liturgy. A Study Book of the Federation of Diocesan Liturgical Commissions, 1982.

Timmons, Gary. *Welcome.* New York: Paulist Press, 1982.

Upton, Julia, R.S.M. "Formation in the RCIA and Religious Communities," *The Chicago Catechumenate,* Volume 5, Number 5, July 1983, pp. 6–11.

Vawter, Bruce, C.M. "Johannine Theology," *The Jerome Biblical Commentary,* Volume II, pp. 828–839. Raymond E. Brown, S.S., Joseph A. Fitzmyer, S.J., and Roland E. Murphy, O.Carm., editors. Englewood Cliffs: Prentice-Hall, Inc., 1968.

————. "The Gospel According to John," *The Jerome Biblical Commentary,* Volume II, pp. 414–466. Raymond E. Brown, S.S., Joseph A. Fitzmyer, S.J., and Roland E. Murphy, O.Carm., editors. Englewood Cliffs: Prentice-Hall, Inc., 1968.

Wiles, Maurice. *The Christian Fathers.* (*Knowing Christianity Series*) Philadelphia: J.B. Lippincott Company, 1966.

Yarnold, Edward, S.J. *The Awe Inspiring Rites of Initiation: Baptismal Homilies of the Fourth Century.* Slough, England: St. Paul Publications, 1971.